Glitch Art in Theory and Practice

Glitch Art in Theory and Practice: Critical Failures and Post-Digital Aesthetics explores the concept of "glitch" alongside Contemporary digital political economy to develop a general theory of critical media using glitch as a case study and model, focusing specifically on examples of digital art and aesthetics. While prior literature on glitch practice in visual arts has been divided between historical discussions and social-political analyses, this work provides a rigorous, contemporary theoretical foundation and framework.

Michael Betancourt is a theorist, historian and artist concerned with digital technology and capitalist ideology. He has been working on the links between theory and practice since 1989, exhibits his movies internationally, and has written several books, including *The Critique of Digital Capitalism; Beyond Spatial Montage: Windowing, or, the Cinematic Displacement of Time, Motion and Space;* and *The History of Motion Graphics: From Avant-Garde to Industry in the United States*. His writing has been translated into Chinese, French, Greek, Italian, Japanese, Persian, Portuguese and Spanish.

Glitch Art in Theory and Practice

Critical Failures and Post-Digital Aesthetics

Michael Betancourt

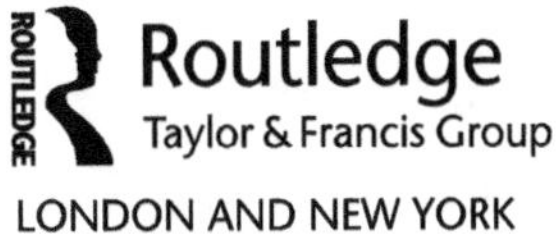
LONDON AND NEW YORK

First published 2017 by Routledge

2 Park Square, Milton Park, Abingdon, Oxfordshire OX14 4RN
52 Vanderbilt Avenue, New York, NY 10017

Routledge is an imprint of the Taylor & Francis Group, an informa business

First issued in paperback 2019

The discussion of Digital TV Dinner in Chapter 1 was published in abridged form in Millennium Film Journal no. 46, Fall 2016 as "The Invention of Glitch Video."

The discussion of Michael Morris's Second and Third Hermeneutics appeared in abridged form in Film International, 2016.

Other discussions first appeared in Bright Lights Film Journal:

"Technology and Transcendence: Prisoner's Cinema by Joshua Gen Solondz," July 26, 2015.

"Dread Mechanics: The Sublime Terror of Decasia," January 14, 2015.

Library of Congress Cataloging-in-Publication Data
A catalog record for this book has been requested

ISBN: 978-1-138-21954-0 (hbk)
ISBN: 978-0-367-88424-6 (pbk)

Typeset in Times New Roman
by Apex CoVantage, LLC

For Leah

Contents

List of Figures viii

Introduction 1

1 Origins of "Glitch" in *The Stoppage* 21

2 The Heritage of Materialist Media 49

3 Digital *Mis*function and Materialist Approaches 80

4 Critical Engagements with Failure 102

Prospects 123

Glossary 133
Index 137

Figures

Frontis	*Sinking Venus—Glitched* (2015) from *Two Women and a Nightengale* by Michael Betancourt	x
0.1	*Mae Murray* (2013), by Michael Betancourt	2
0.2a	Stills from *Malfunction* (2000) glitched SD video by Michael Betancourt	4
0.2b	Stills showing different types of glitches appearing in HD video	5
1.1	Typed title card for *Digital TV Dinner* from *EVE3* (1978)	25
1.2	Title card for *Digital TV Dinner* from *Image Union,* Episode 11 (1979)	26
1.3	"Audio by Dick Ainsworth" title card for *Digital TV Dinner* from *Image Union,* Episode 11 (1979)	26
1.4	Title card for *Grafix* from *Image Union,* Episode 11 (1979)	28
1.5	Repeating graphic elements characteristic of visual glitches	33
1.6	Still from *Monster Movie* (2005), by Takeshi Murata	36
1.7	Menu from the *Bally Astrocade* appearing in *Digital TV Dinner* (1978)	39
1.8	Boot screen logos for the *Bally Astrocade* appearing in *Digital TV Dinner* (1978)	40
1.9	Stills from *Digital TV Dinner* (1978) showing "Select Game" text	41
1.10	Still from the "Gunfight" game appearing in *Grafix* from *Image Union,* Episode 11 (1979)	42
1.11	"Game Over" text from *Digital TV Dinner* (1978)	43

1.12a Error message: "Unplayable video file" 44
1.12b Error message: "The movie could not be opened" 44
1.12c Error message: "The connection was reset" 45
2.1 Still from *Prisoner's Cinema* (2012), by Joshua Gen Solondz 68
2.2 Still from *Prisoner's Cinema* (2012), by Joshua Gen Solondz 70
3.1 Screen and projectors from *Second Hermeneutic* (2013), by Michael Morris 81
3.2 Interlaced film projections from *Second Hermeneutic* (2013), by Michael Morris 83
3.3 Custom audio patch in Pd used in *Third Hermeneutic* (2014), by Michael Morris 84
3.4 *Glitched Allegory of the Knight, Death and Durer* (2013), by Michael Betancourt 97
4.1 Text reading "Begin Lamentation" from *zijkfijergijok* (2002), by the artist collective reMI (Renate Oblak and Michael Pinter) 107
4.2 Raul Marks, human face from *Halt and Catch Fire* (2014) 109
4.3 Crossing the barrier from *Halt and Catch Fire* (2014) 111
4.4 Human outline figure from *Halt and Catch Fire* (2014) 111
4.5 Film decay from *Decasia* (2002), by Bill Morrison 114
4.6 Still from *Decasia* (2002), by Bill Morrison 117
4.7 Man apparently interacting with the visual results of decay in *Decasia* (2002), by Bill Morrison 118
4.8 Spinning dervish from *Decasia* (2002), by Bill Morrison 119
4.9 Solarized image of weavers from *Decasia* (2002), by Bill Morrison 120
4.10 Man boxing with film decay from *Decasia* (2002), by Bill Morrison 121
5.1 Still from *Going Somewhere* (2016), by Michael Betancourt 124

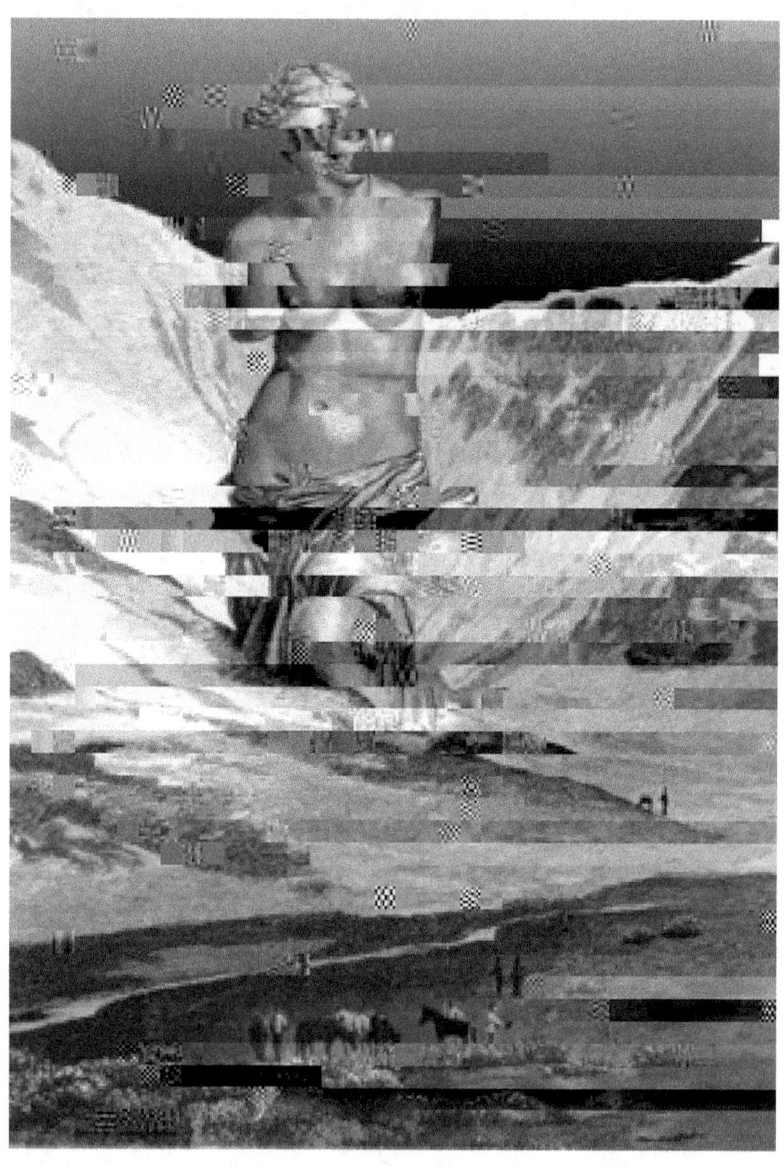

Frontis Sinking Venus—Glitched (2015) from *Two Women and a Nightengale* by Michael Betancourt

Introduction

This book originated with a short discussion of the problematics around "glitch art" as an inherently critical media practice. My article "Critical Glitches and Glitch Art" published in 2014 by the Swedish art and music journal *Hz,* is the foundation for the current discussion of Contemporary questions of "critical media." The question that animates this study, "At what point does an interventionist or hacker aesthetic become a political gesture or institutional critique rather than being recuperated as trendy Formalist technique?", challenges our Contemporary theoretical apparatus that claims we must not (or cannot) separate generation from reception in determining the correct ways to interpret that work. It is primarily concerned with the heritage of avant-garde or experimental film and expanded cinema as it becomes Contemporary digital video heuristics. Making this argument requires a reassessment of what the Contemporary has declared historical; any unconscious vacillation over the relationship between the Modern and the Contemporary is apt to lead to confusion about what this book argues for and against. Rather than finding a singular answer to these problematics, this book seeks a discursive revaluation of the ongoing influence Theodor Adorno's Modernist aesthetics and formal considerations have on critical heuristics. These approaches, commonly assigned a marginal position in relation to art theory and commercial cinema, are also commonly considered *critical* forms of praxis, engaged and challenging the more common, "dominant" cinema. This critical semiosis renders questions of origins (generation) as themselves interpretations, a recognition that also challenges the Marxist aspects of the theorization of critical media practice, opening a chasm between the digital source (generation) and its reception (interpretation).

1

"Glitch" may be best known from its role in electronic music and digital composition, but it is equally—and more commonly—a part of the everyday visual engagement with computers. The technical aspects of digital

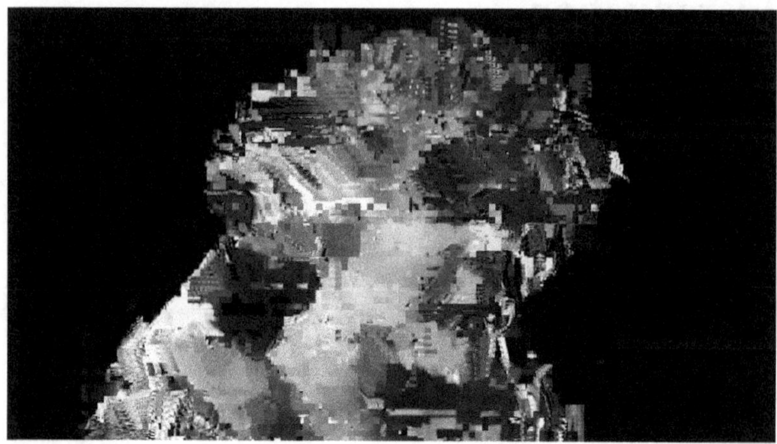

Figure 0.1 *Mae Murray* (2013), by Michael Betancourt

technology—pixelated images that re/compose reality as a juxtaposition of discrete fragments—suggests a translation of visual space into a virtuality, *cyberspace*, that instead of being continuous is shot through with errors and failures of various types. [Figure 0.1] Transfers between this digital technology and art have been a continuous part of its history, but the prominence of digital imagery and digitally derived forms has become an insistent part of Contemporary media since the popular embrace of the Internet in the mid-1990s. These visual forms of glitch, unlike its musical counterparts, have consistently been grouped with a variety of other terms, prominent among these are post-digital, post-internet and the new aesthetic; in academic contexts visual glitch will often simply be identified with new media art, or occasionally video art.

In profiling the work of predominantly UK artists in 2011, *IDN* magazine defined glitch not in terms of its failure, but as the embrace of these malfunctions:

> It started out as a software malfunction—not it is a design genre. Instead of holding their hands up in horror and crying: "Oh, oh, we have a glitch!" the artists featured in this article say "Whoopee! We have a glitch!"—and proceed to make the most of it.[1]

The artist/designers profiled include familiar names: Benjamin Gaulon, Chris Seddon, Clement Valla, Justin Blyth, Kim Asendorf, Misha Shyukin,

Olivier Ratsi, Quayola, Rob Sheridan, Roger de Boeve, Sebastian Onufszak and Tokyo22. This popular coverage, accompanied by a DVD of videos, is focused on the transformation of familiar technical failures into graphics whose distinction from the graphic design of the magazine itself is often blurred: it can be hard to distinguish magazine layout from its glitch contents. Iman Moradi identified the visual features of these failures in *Glitch Aesthetics* as a discrete collection of morphologies: fragmentation, replication/repetition, and linearity.[2] The integration of glitch into graphic design as a specific visual style places the digital malfunction in a continuum with other types of malfunctions such as misregistered color separations in printing.

However, an engagement with the visual products of computational processes is not enough to define the glitch. It is specifically the result of aberrant and apparent "abnormal" renderings by digital technology that are of interest. The complexities of these identifications, as David Barry and Michael Dieter note in the introduction to their anthology *Postdigital Aesthetics* (2015), that "the everyday experience of life within computal societies inspires a search for new concepts and experience, or perhaps 'formal indicators' as vague neologisms, in an attempt to historically delimit and define the present."[3] The varied terminologies and approaches identifying the emergent digital as a dominant cultural model reflect the difficulties they describe. The designation "glitch" occupies a prominent place within the "formal indicators" describing the transition from a world identified with continuity and the pixelated, sampled world familiar from digital screens. In *Postdigital Aesthetics* historians Christiane Paul and Malcom Levy explain the scope of these formal elements' emergence in art:

> The terms "glitch" and "corruption artifacts" in the broadest sense refer to images and objects that have been tampered with; their creation relates to the core of the media apparatuses used to store, produce and relay information. These corrupted images can be created by adjusting or manipulating the normal physical or virtual composition of the machine or software itself, or by using machines or digital tools in methods different from their normative modalities.[4]

Glitch procedures engage and reflect technical failures in digital systems—one is tempted to describe glitch as "courting disaster"—since the results of these processes verge on a complete systemic/structural failure [Figure 0.2 a and b]. These same transient failures employed as aesthetic material were discussed in 2000 by Kim Casone's earlier article in *Computer Music Journal*. "The Aesthetics of Failure: 'Post-Digital' Tendencies in Contemporary

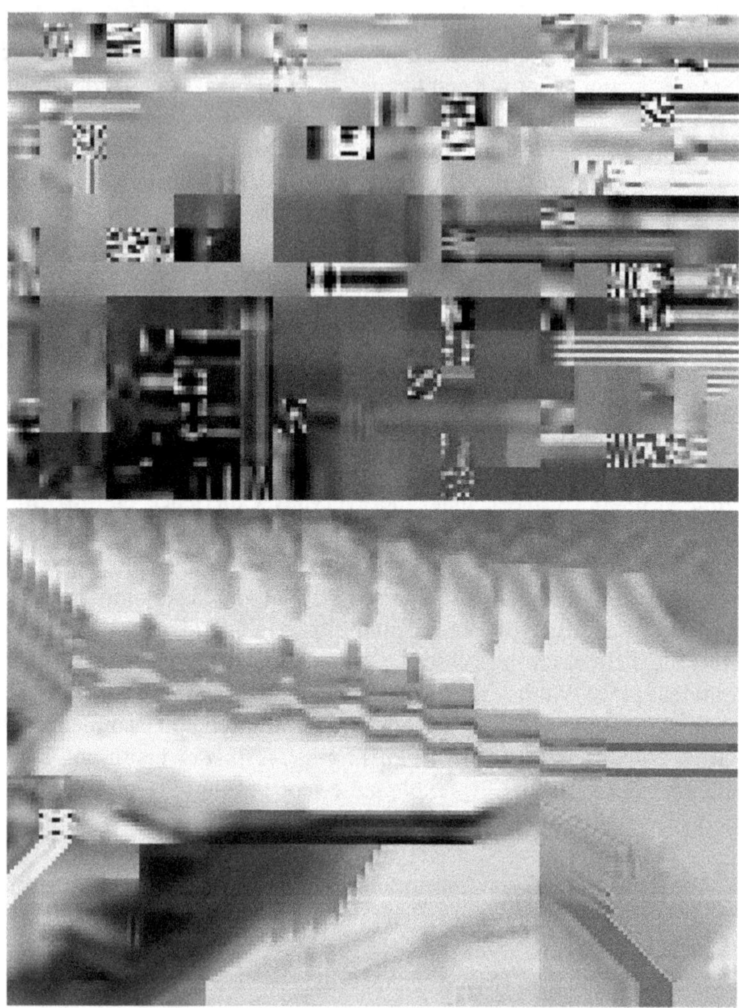

Figure 0.2a Stills from *Malfunction* (2000) glitched SD video by Michael Betancourt © 2000 Michael Betancourt/Artists Rights Society (ARS)

Music" proposed glitches as a material element that he identified with the procedural basis of digital media—the digital is generated autonomously:

> The "post-digital" aesthetic was developed in part as a result of the immersive experience of working in environments suffused with digital technology: computer fans whirring, laser printers churning out

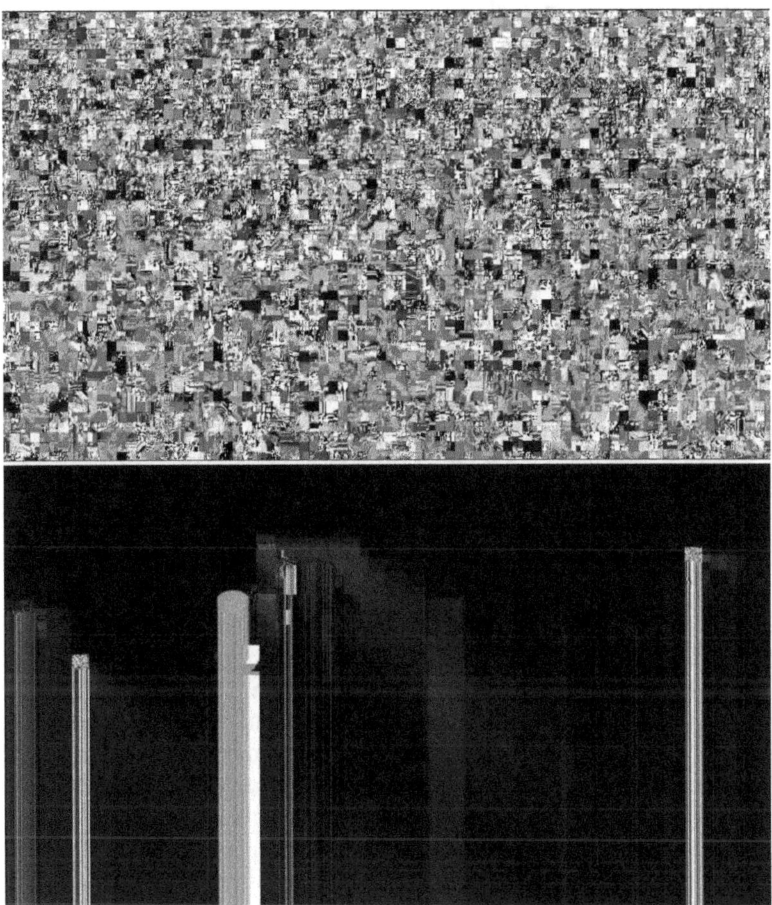

Figure 0.2b Stills showing different types of glitches appearing in HD video

> documents, the sonification of user-interfaces, and the muffled noise of hard drives. But more specifically, it is from the "failure" of digital technology that this new work has emerged: glitches, bugs, application errors, system crashes, clipping,aliasing, distortion, quantization noise, and even the noise floor of computer sound cards are the raw materials composers seek to incorporate intotheir music.[5]

The list that Cascone identifies is not limited to technical failures, but includes a range of physical elements that might be equally categorized as intrusions upon the idealized encounter with a digital work; his designation of these as post-digital reflects their emergence *after* the action of the digital machine (or perhaps in excess to it). His list collectively describes those elements which accompany immaterial digital production, but are indicative of its physical, material nature. They are formal indicators of computational action, the noise that surrounds and arises from the operation of hardware and software.

The ascendant prominence of this noise follows the logic in philosopher Jacques Attali's argument about the domestication of noise effected by music, in the control exercised by recording:

> With noise is born disorder and its opposite: the world. With music is born power and its opposite: subversion. In noise can be read the codes of life, the relations among them. Clamor, Melody, Dissonance, harmony; when it is fashioned by man with specific tools, when it invades man's time, when it becomes sound, noise is the source of purpose and power, of the dream—music.[6]

Applying Attali's theory of noise to a definition of glitch offers an understanding of their potential for transgression in the violation of the established codes of perception and order (Attali relies on earlier aesthetic theory by Theodor Adorno to develop this critical dialectic,[7] which will be considered in Chapter 2). The material markers that Cascone lists as elements in the digital glitch music have visual analogues—but their imagistic counterparts are precisely those elements typically ignored when encountered. Their shift in focus from the periphery to being central to the work is a particular attempt to counter the tendency to ignore the glitch, to cast it out of consciousness. Attali's concept of noise also contains the seed of its elision—the order he identifies rejects these elements, rather than engaging or even acknowledging their presence—glitches are part of our Contemporary digital media experience that appear not as a violation of media's perfection, but as transient surface flaws that rapidly vanish from both our screens and our consideration. Their banality as well as insignificance in relation to the actual foci of interest, the information they accompany, renders them forgotten almost instantly after they have passed.

Following Attali, Cascone conceptualizes a critical role for glitches appearing in the work of composers such as Ryoji Ikeda. The network of historical and ideological foundations that are common to the digital as a whole encourages an interpretation of these glitches as indicative of the materially of the digital technology—elements that are rapidly discarded as extraneous; thus glitch elements are "background"—as the elided part of the encounter and interpretation:

> The basic composition of "background" is comprised of data we filter out to focus on our immediate surroundings. The data hidden in our perceptual "blind spot" contains worlds waiting to be explored, if we choose to shift our focus there.[8]

The invisibility Cascone identifies with digital glitches is the aura of the digital in action, the stripping of these physical elements of digital media as simply epiphenomena. Constructing a critical analysis of glitch thus requires a consideration of the ideological apparatus built up around and supported by digital technology, a rejection of the aura of the digital, that recognizes how digital machines instantiate the assumptions and foundations of capitalism in instrumental form; however, these critical interpretations of glitch are also inherently problematic because the vehicle of this critical engagement—the glitches—*rupture* only the apparently seamless media experience under specific and limited circumstances. The tendency, as Cascone notes, is to identify them as background, a dismissal as superficial flaws of the immanent encounter, *not* as significant material demonstration that requires further analysis or interpretation. This is what the designation "glitch" commonly signifies: a lack of significance, that it is background to be elided from consideration.

That the digital object is completely distinct from the instantiation of it in some physical form makes the idealization that is foundational for the aura of the digital seem immanent, paradoxically realized in the immaterial digital file itself. The glitch as epiphenomenal asserts an absolute difference between the physical encounter and the digital itself: this transcendent ideal applied to digital technology is the aura of the digital; it has an "aura of information" composed from both a machine-generated and a human-readable work created by the computer from a digital file (itself actually stored in some type of physical media).

Material dimensions of glitch enable a reappropriation of historical production that is easily associated with earlier fetishes of the artist's "hand" in historically materialist art. The material features of historical cinema (camera, lenses, graininess, flicker) draws attention to the mechanical photographic medium itself; a similar collection of features could be readily identified for digital media, including but not limited to resolution, compression, artifacts—as well as technical errors of all types in any reproduction technology—the same elements Cascone listed. The challenge to capitalism seemingly posed by these material markers has a specific historical lineage originating in an ironic semiotics of "skilled craft" common to the nineteenth century Arts and

Crafts movements and their heritage: the appearance of visible brush strokes, imperfections and natural variation in manufacture such as hammer marks or bubbles, that were the historical signs of unskilled labor.[9] These lists of material markers allude/claim to evoke the physicality of production—both glitch and other historical errors of film parallel the opposition to the idealized/supposed perfection of machined production in the Arts and Crafts' productions. Continuity with the material world has been systematically obscured by the fantasy that digital production is fundamentally and categorically different from the historical physical production of industrial capitalism. The shift from human to digital labor is the historical result of industrial capitalism's attempts to replace the variable costs of labor with the fixed costs of machinery. These analogues for the material markers of production in the immaterial visual shifts the form but not the historical critique of capitalism's deskilling of production and labor towards an embrace of unintelligent, unskilled labor that can readily be replaced by automation.[10]

Digital capitalism emerges as human labor is replaced by machines capable of increasingly sophisticated actions—ones that historically required the intelligent labor of humans but which digital automation can now perform faster, cheaper and more consistently, producing a dematerialization of value into the immaterial production philosopher Katerina Kolozova explains in *Towards a Radical Metaphysics of Socialism*:

> There is nothing material in the 21st century's form of capitalism. Contemporary capitalism is not only based on "immaterial labor," as Negri and Hardt claim, but also on pure abstraction and elevation to the immateriality of both labor and capital. This situation is the result of the complete mathematization and speculation of the real.[11]

The transition to digital capitalism is a dissolution of concerns with physicality and a denial of material basis. The glitch can act as a stoppage of this autonomous production, a transitory failure whose critical potential depends on violating this aura of the digital. Glitch, in this interruptive role, suggests the materiality of media, offering the potential for a transition into a critique of digital capitalism, requiring a refusal of mystification: the productive, material and historical connections between industrial capitalism and digital capitalism proceed from a matrix of precise control that connects the seemingly immaterial action of autonomous machinery to earlier protocols of industrial production that rendered their (necessary) human labor unintelligent. *How* glitch can achieve this making-conscious is the problem posed by the aura of the digital stripping of any and all temporary interruptions from consciousness as merely an epiphenomenon, without significance. There is no easy or simple solution to this problem; simply employing glitch in media work does not automatically produce a critical meaning or engaged response.

Visual, audible and interactive glitches are united by being "technical failures," the parallel considerations of glitches in digital music and interactivity (internet and game-based glitches), or metaphorically as cultural descriptor rather than particular aesthetic phenomenon, have created a critical lacuna around visual glitch in relation to earlier materialist engagements with visual media. The limited engagement with visual glitches by academics is countered by an abundance of theoretical and critical work by the artists themselves. Cascone identified this duality of academic analysis and Contemporary practice that is a feature of glitch in digital music as well:

> Over the past decade, [the 1990s] the Internet has helped spawn a new movement in digital music. It is not academically based, and for the most part the composers involved are self-taught. Music journalists occupy themselves inventing names for it, and some have already taken root: glitch, microwave, DSP, sinecore, and microscopic music. These names evolved through a collection of deconstructive audio and visual techniques that allow artists to work beneath the previously impenetrable veil of digital media.[12]

The heuristic element of glitch theory has developed among artists; the academic theorization and conceptualization of glitch takes developments in digital music as an implicit reference point; an expansion of these concerns is apparent throughout Mark Nunes's book *Noise Channels* and in Caleb Kelly's *Cracked Media: The Sound of Malfunction*, both of which are primarily concerned with glitches in music. While their considerations included some consideration of visual glitches, this analysis is focused on visual work. It elides the differences to develop the productive relationship between glitches and avant-garde film and video art.

2

Positing "critical media practice" necessarily implies a political component to the works in question; in the ascription of a critical meaning to glitch, the development and context of digital capitalism becomes central to this analysis: the question "how can glitches produce a critical media practice?" leads to the problematics of the digital itself and its relationship to capitalism[13]—the same historical questions that any critical media practice engages—opening the implications of this critique beyond its primary focus on visual glitches: the key term in approaching and understanding critical media practice is not the critical, but the practice. The relationships between historical Formalism, Modernism, and the Contemporary questions of generation, interpretation and production construct the parameters *for* critical practice. In consequence, this examination engages the heuristic theories and engagements of artists working with glitch as they develop from and intersect with earlier theoretical approaches to critical media, in particular those derived from Marxist analysis. The context for this consideration is thus not entirely the academic realm of critical hermeneutics, but rather their more limited, dynamic intersection with practice.

Informing these heuristics are the connections between industrial and digital capitalism. The "control revolution" that links them presents significant continuities emergent as historical industrial production developed into digital capitalism. The emergence of digital capitalism follows from earlier developments displacing human labor in the productive process. Kolozova identifies this apparatus as dependent on the control deployed through production:

> The cruelty of capitalism consists in the capacity to fully rationalize any suffering of the body as well as the relentless exploitation of all organic life. The absolute rule over humanity and its reason is no different than the rule of Hegel's Spirit whose aim is not only the absolute subjugation of Nature, but also its destruction in the name of "pure reason." This apocalyptic eschatological vision is explicitly advocated in the *Phenomenology of the Spirit.*[14]

As capitalist production methods mature, they increasingly reflect a controlling formal analysis that isolates the essential elements of value and eliminates everything else. The development of digital capitalism thus begins much earlier with *Taylorism*, named for Frederick W. Taylor, the engineer who codified the scientific approach to business management. The implementation of Taylorism by Henry Ford created the assembly line and enabled the mass production that defined industrial capitalism in the first half of the twentieth century. *The Principles of Scientific Management* (1911) approached manufacturing as an engineering problem where the human element was the point-of-failure, the source of glitches in the result:

> The work of every workman is fully planned out . . . describing in detail the task which he is to accomplish as well as the means to be used in doing the work.[15]

By removing the worker's engagement in deciding the methods for doing a task and replacing those choices with a methodology produced through an empirical study it would be possible to increase efficiency enormously; a critical analysis that seeks to isolate and identify the essential actions for production, and become reified as the autonomous semiotic (and algorithmically determined) production via the organization and structure of cybernetics: the translation of this approach into an algorithm enables the elimination of human labor entirely and its replacement by digital technology.

The abstraction and narrowing of potentials in this capitalist protocol parallels the Modernist search for pure aesthetic forms, a transfer from industrial production into aesthetics that reveals the common foundation of Hegel described by Kolozova. This scientific production converges with Clement Greenberg's description of a Kantian "self-criticism" in his 1961 essay "Modernist Painting," presenting the link between aesthetics and capitalist production is a function of their reliance on the same reductive philosophical foundations:

> The self-criticism of Modernism grows out of, but is not the same as, the criticism of the Enlightenment. The Enlightenment criticized from the outside, the way criticism in its accepted sense does; Modernism criticized from the inside, through the procedures themselves of that which is being criticized.[16]

Both Taylor's scientific management and Greenberg's proposal of self-criticism are demonstrative of a common ideological foundation[17]; despite of their many differences, both theories employ the same procedures of reification, elision and reduction: "purity." His process reveals how its basic tautological organization renders it apparently neutral, a necessary and logical deduction:

> The essence of Modernism lies, as I see it, in the use of characteristic methods of a discipline to criticize the discipline itself, not in order to subvert it but in order to entrench it more firmly in its area of competence. [. . .] What had to be exhibited was not only that which was unique and irreducible in art in general, but also that which was unique and irreducible in each particular art.[18]

Identifying the "characteristic methods" essential to Greenberg's conception of purity begins a reductive process that identifies the essential components of any given medium based on an *a priori* definition that justifies their selection based on the results of their use: it is a tautological approach that reifies its selection of components, then justifies that choice by the "characteristic methods" correspondence to the definition used for their selection: they are both demonstration of and evidence arguing for that definition. Once this initial tautology is set in motion, these elements become self-reinforcing emblems for the independence and self-referential isolation of the medium the both demonstrate and define: their role is semiotic as the specific signs of that medium; Greenberg's aesthetic is transferred to avant-garde film in the later 1960s and 1970s.

By considering how machine labor as an extension of human action—as the mechanical amplification of human labor—becomes the digital, the machine does not augment but supplant. This removal of the human intermediary whose importance Taylorism removes from production (assembly-line labor is instrumental, not intelligent) is part of a continuous trajectory from tasks organized around repetitive action (itself an organization that implies semiotic disassembly and standardization) into the automation of actions in digital automation where computers leave only a limited role for humans. For Taylor's analysis the human decision is the problem to be removed from the production process, just as human labor (in the form of wages) is the expense that must be minimized to maintain profitability. The capacity for alienation that emerges from the psychological distance of capitalist production, as art historian Renato Poggioli noted about the historical avant-garde, provides a model for a critical conception of glitches:

> The state of alienation must first of all be considered a psychological alienation [. . .] caused by a process of social degeneration, an ineluctable crisis of a society unable to die or to renew itself [. . .] as the feeling of uselessness and isolation to a person who has lost its sense of the human condition and its own historical mission.[19]

Alienation emerges within this framework as the expression of a set of semiotic codes that are indifferent to an established order; these altered codes are recognizable from the vertigo they can provoke. The emergence of digital technology (and by extension digital capitalism) is *not* a rupture with the historical processes of industrial capitalism but an amplification of its priorities reified in the productive methods and fragmentary protocols of industrial manufacturing.

Scientific management requires an active suppression of intelligent action by human labor, replaced by a rote, unintelligent process, one immediately recognizable as contiguous with the action of the digital, revealing the direct link between the industrial assembly line and autonomous machines. This fragmentation into discrete, quantified units that enable a specific type of discursive and analytic action informs the cybernetic approach, explained by the British pioneer of cybernetics William Ross Ashby in his book *Introduction to Cybernetics* with as fragmentation. This approach clarifies and strengthens its conception through a process of refinement: it is not the vast differences between Ashby, Greenberg and Taylor, but their convergence in a logic of control and restriction that reveals the pervasive impact of capitalist eventualities:

> Often a change occurs continuously, that is, by infinitesimal steps, as when the earth moves through space, or a sunbather's skin darkens under exposure. The consideration of steps that are infinitesimal, however, raises a number of purely mathematical difficulties, so we shall avoid their consideration entirely. Instead, we shall assume in all cases that the changes occur by finite steps in time and that any difference is also finite. We shall assume that the change occurs by a measurable jump, as the money in a bank account changes by at least a penny. Though this supposition may seem artificial in a world in which continuity is common, it has great advantages in an Introduction and is not as artificial as it seems. When the differences are finite, all the important questions, as we shall see later, can be decided by simple counting, so that it is easy to be quite sure whether we are right or not. Were we to consider continuous changes we would often have to compare infinitesimal against infinitesimal, or to consider what we would have after adding together an infinite number of infinitesimals—questions by no means easy to answer.[20]

Ashby's process of rationalization is a productive model of sampling and isolation that unifies the industrial fragmentation of the assembly line with the protocols of digital automation. Control is the focus. Predetermined rules for assembly and permutation assume the same productive role as the fragmentation of physical action into discrete, sequential tasks. Control follows from an *a priori* definition where the identification of procedures depends on the *results to be produced.* It is not a "given." This protocol produces radically different results depending on how the object being examined has been defined: the results are logical, but also fully contingent on the initial conditions of the analysis; at the same time, it alienates that work from its functional and historical context, allowing a limited range of technical and aesthetic propositions and eliminating the others as "external."

The claims of rupture with physical and historical models common to the aura of the digital acts to obscure this common foundation, enabling the fantasy of the digital as a self-productive domain independent of historical processes and earlier capitalism. This recognition counters the rhetoric of disruption accompanying the aura of the digital's separation of physical and immaterial, revealing digital automation as an amplification that enacts the same elision of human agency as the industrial assembly line. The Contemporary reflects an internalization of these demands, as well as a reification of earlier capitalist priorities. In exploring these relationships and history in media art—experimental film, video art and new media—the role of digital capitalism emerges as an invisible, ubiquitous influence that demonstrates the difficulties for a critical media practice must also address implicit reiterations at both the heuristic level of praxis and in the theorization of that practice.

3

The particular configuration of the Contemporary period reflects not only the assimilation of Post-Modernist critiques and the rejection of the futurity of the historical avant-garde, but a ratification of Modernism as an ongoing, interminable present. This conception of the "Contemporary" by critics such as Terry Smith and C. B. Johnson coincides with the programmatic aspects of Contemporary capitalism and the ideology of an "end to history" that supports this political economy. As Smith describes in "Contemporary Art and Contemporaneity," the ubiquitous force determinant of the *shape* of the Contemporary is linked to economic power:

> contemporary art, as a movement, has become the new Modern, or, what amounts to the same thing, the old Modern in new clothes. In its most institutionalized forms—from the triumphalist overreach of the Guggenheim Museum's global franchising through the Old Master elegance of the installations at Dia:Beacon to the confused gesturing in the contemporary galleries when the Museum of Modern Art, New York, reopened in 2004—it is the latest phase in the century-and-a-half-long story of Modern art in Europe and its cultural colonies, a continuation of the Modernist lineage, warily selected not least in an attempt to preserve this cultural balance of power.[21]

The balance of power Smith describes is one closely aligned with the transformations and global reach of cultural allegiances reflecting the impact of a networked distribution system that enables the continuous flow of information-power demonstrated by/through the art world's global reach. That these centers of this Contemporary power remain the same as those in the twentieth century—yet rendered global in reach—reveal linkages between the cultural domains and the economic ones; cultural authority thus reiterates the structure of economic power. Johnson's proposal in *Modernity without a Project: Essays on the Void called Contemporary,* describes this network of cultural and social forces; the approach to "Contemporariness" employed by Smith and Johnson implies the transformative effects of digital technology whose semiotic protocols are the productive dimensions of digital capitalism. The same network dominates cultural, economic and productive domains; this structure emerges from the fantasies that developed around digital technology, what as I proposed in my article "The Aura of the Digital" as

> the illusion of a self-productive domain, infinite, capable of creating value without expenditure, unlike the reality of limited resources, time, expense, etc. that otherwise govern all forms of value and production. [. . .] The aura of the digital signals the digital as the site of a specific reification dramatizing an underlying conflict between production and consumption within capitalism itself—that is, between the accumulation of capital and its expenditure. By enabling the fantasy of accumulation without consumption, digital technology becomes an ideological force reifying the conflict between the limits imposed on the value of capital via expenditure and inflation, and the demand implicit in the capitalist ideology of escalating value. [. . .] Digital technology, its development, deployment, production and access all demand a large expenditure of capital both to create and to maintain. The aura of the digital separates the results from its technological foundation.[22]

Digital capitalism emerges from the same cultural balance of power that Johnson describes, a continuation of structural authority apparent in historical capitalism itself. The convergence of cultural and economic forces unites the Contemporary cultural power structure with the dominant organization and flows of digital capitalism—flows hidden by the aura of the digital where results are separated from their proximate, physical causes, a separation that originates with the rupture specific to the aura of the digital. Physical constraints are elided in favor of a transcendent belief in immaterial abundance.

The problem for a critical practice in digital media as well as a theory of that practice begins with the ways this heritage has been reified as the technology itself: the rise of these semiotic procedures during the Post-Modern in the art world accompany the rise to dominance of digital capitalism during these same decades. Both are symptom-effects demonstrating the same semiotic approach to interpretation being applied in parallel and ultimately converging domains, the cultural and the economic.

4

Other considerations of glitch, such as that proposed by Tim Barker in his article in *Error: Glitch, Noise and Jam in New Media Cultures*, seek to construct a general philosophy of errors in art, one that reveals their focus on the autonomous generative parameters—the origins of the failure:

> The idea of *degrees of freedom* comes from Manual De Landa's work on the philosophy of science. This concept with De Landa takes from

> the discipline of mathematics, refers to the ways in which an object may change. For instance, he gives the example of a pendulum, which, as it can only ever change its velocity and its position has two degrees of freedom. [. . .] The degrees of freedom are thus the limits in which a system unfolds; they are the boundaries that direct the process of the system. Transplanting this thinking to the aesthetics of the machine and the aesthetics of error, we see that aesthetic processes are an output of a particular condition that is set up by the artist. [. . .] Post-digital cultural communication can now be considered as SENDER—SOFTWARE—MESSAGE—SOFTWARE—RECEIVER. In this model, the cultural significance of software is emphasized. The software, much more than the noise introduced by the communication channel, may change the message. Significantly, the software may introduce an error into the message.[23]

The element of interpretation by the audience (receiver) engaging the object in Barker's description is only present *en passant*—instead, the interpretive engagement is handled in an idealized fashion: the mediating role of software seems to supplant (or replace) the mediating role of *human* interpretation. This post-digital cultural communication is one that elides the essential human component in exactly the same way that rationalization reduces human involvement in production, the same emphasis on the replacement of human action by autonomous processes (in this case software) acts to shift the critical focus away from the interpretative engagement to a mechanically predictable process described in advance by the machine's degrees of freedom, a construction that elides the human engagement for a reified critical demonstration, *glitch.*

The appearance of "glitch" as a term describing aesthetic and artistic embrace of this post-digital—the physical context and materiality of digital generation—unifies the descriptor "glitch" across digital media works attempting a critical practice. The underlying problem posed by the aura of the digital is the close correspondence between historical magic and the claims for/about Contemporary digital technology: that the digital presents an illusion of a self-productive domain, infinite, capable of creating value without expenditure, reflected by the seeming perfection and idealization assigned to digital objects, whatever their physical form's shortcomings might be. The apparent linkage of generation and reception that glitch implies is a false unity, as Chapters 2 and 3 will show: the problem lies specifically with determining "origin." This conclusion is itself an interpretation depending on the reception of digital media that is entirely generative, unlike analogue media where a physical support can be understood as both containing and presenting the media work, this distinction is paradoxically both simultaneously absolute and uncertain with digital media: the difference between the generated elements and those that are ruptures are products of audience interpretation.

Historical links between art theory and industrial protocols inform the development of digital technology and complicate the reception/interpretation of it in media art. Glitch thus seems to offer an escape from the ideology of automation's expanding force by revealing the misfunction of the digital machine—but this apparent avenue of escape is problematic: it assumes the underlying ideological functions of the digital remain unchanged, offering instead a momentary potential for rupture. Understanding and addressing this dynamic, as well as the resilience of the digital as ideological form, are the issues this book seeks to investigate.

"Being critical," however, has historically been conceived as a material function of the work in question, an innate quality that defines the meaning in advance and against any other potential interpretations—these problematics are developed in more detail in Chapters 2 and 3. The claim that glitches are an inherently critical form is a function of this historical theoretical foundation continuing to structure and organize the Contemporary. The continuing role for Modernism that Terry Smith and C.B. Johnson describe is an answer to the question of if the avant-garde is the *advance force*, what is it in advance of? The Contemporary necessitates historical engagement precisely because the ahistorical nowness of digital capitalism acts to deny continuities between earlier capitalist organization of labor and production and those specific to digital technology.

It is precisely the contention that the Contemporary is *not* a continuation of Modernism which this analysis challenges—in the process proposing an alternative to these formal approaches that structure Contemporary interpretations of glitch. The continuity of historical concerns and prescriptions with critical interpretations of media—most apparent in the claims that some media are easier or harder to recuperate, to tame, to claim or recuperate—is precisely the ideological construct critiqued by considering its roots: Chapter 1 discusses historical origins of digital video glitches and their relationship to later work; Chapter 2 considers the links between glitches and earlier Formalist media theory; Chapter 3 concerns the role of digital capitalism in the consideration of digital media; Chapter 4 considers a dynamic model of interpretation focused by the human engagement with the work in determining it to be critical; Prospects surveys the network of connections and critical engagements this analysis proposes. Many concepts reappear in different chapters, each time being developed and addressed in different ways meant to develop a more dimensional understanding.

The critique of digital media proposed in this book develops around video glitches; in place of a singular, definitive answer, this analysis seeks a range of potentials for understanding them—some of which have a critical potential dependent on the interpreting, human audience. In place of following the temptation to develop and present a solution in the form of definitive protocols and techniques for producing a critical media, this study takes a theoretical approach that investigates and considers the connections between the technical protocol that is glitch and the embeddedness of this practice within a larger network of conceptual and theoretical issues constrains its critical potentials.

Notes

1. "The Glitch Issue: Making the Perfect Accident" in *IDN: International Design Network Magazine*, Vol. 18, No. 3 (2011) np.
2. Moradi, Iman. *Gltch Aesthetics* (BA dissertation, School of Design Technology, Department of Architecture, The University of Huddersfield, January 27, 2004) pp. 28–33.
3. Berry, David M. and Michael Dieter. "Thinking Postdigital Aesthetics: Art, Computation and Design" in *Postdigital Aesthetics: Art, Computation and Design*, eds. David M. Berry and Michael Dieter (New York: Palmgrave Macmillan, 2015) p. 4.
4. Paul, Christiane and Malcom Levy. "Genealogies of the New Aesthetic" in *Postdigital Aesthetics: Art, Computation and Design*, eds. David M. Berry and Michael Dieter (New York: Palmgrave Macmillan, 2015) p. 31.
5. Cascone, Kim. "The Aesthetics of Failure: 'Post-Digital' Tendencies in Contemporary Computer Music" in *Computer Music Journal*, Vol. 24, No. 4 (Winter, 2000) pp. 12–13.
6. Attali, Jacques. *Noise: The Political Economy of Music* (Minneapolis: University of Minnesota Press, 1985) p. 6.
7. Navas, Eduardo. *Remix Theory: The Aesthetics of Sampling* (New York: Springer, 2012) pp. 90–91.
8. Cascone, Kim. "The Aesthetics of Failure: 'Post-Digital' Tendencies in Contemporary Computer Music" in *Computer Music Journal*, Vol. 24, No. 4 (Winter, 2000) pp. 13–14.
9. Edwards, Robert. "The Art of Work" in *The Art That Is Life: The Arts and Crafts Movement in America, 1875–1920*, ed. Wendy Kaplan (Boston: Museum of Fine Arts, 1987) pp. 234–235.
10. As Marx notes, the "labor power" in question is that of the unskilled, rather than the highly trained: "It is the expenditure of simple labor power, i.e., of the labor power which, on an average, apart from any special development, exists in the organism of every ordinary individual. Simple average labor, it is true, varies in character in different countries and at different times, but in a particular society it is given. Skilled labor counts only as simple labor intensified, or rather, as multiplied simple labor, a given quantity of skilled being considered equal to a greater quantity of simple labor. Experience shows that this reduction is constantly being made. A commodity may be the product of the most skilled labor, but its value, by equating it to the product of simple unskilled labor, represents a definite quantity of the latter labor alone" from *Capital, Volume 1*, Section 2.
11. Kolozova, Katerina. *Towards a Radical Metaphysics of Socialism* (New York: Punctum Books, 2015) p. 41.

12. Cascone, Kim. "The Aesthetics of Failure: 'Post-Digital' Tendencies in Contemporary Computer Music" in *Computer Music Journal*, Vol. 24, No. 4 (Winter, 2000) p. 12.
13. Gournelos, Ted. "Disrupting the Public Sphere: Mediated Noise and Oppositional Politics" in *Error: Glitch Noise and Jam in New Media Cultures*, ed. Mark Nunes (New York: Bloomsbury, 2011) pp. 151–167.
14. Kolozova, Katerina. *Towards a Radical Metaphysics of Socialism* (New York: Punctum Books, 2015) p. 66.
15. Taylor, Frederick. *The Principles of Scientific Management* (New York: Harper, 1911) p. 39.
16. Greenberg, Clement. "Modernist Painting" in *Clem'ent Greenberg: The Collected Essays and Criticism, Volume 4*, ed. John O'Brian (Chicago: University of Chicago Press, 1993) p. 85.
17. Greenberg, Clement. *The Collected Essays and Criticism, Volume 1* (Chicago: University of Chicago Press, 1955) pp. 5–11.
18. Greenberg, Clement. "Modernist Painting" in *Clement Greenberg: The Collected Essays and Criticism, Volume 4*, ed. John O'Brian (Chicago: University of Chicago Press, 1993) p. 85.
19. Poggioli, Renato. *The Theory of the Avant-garde* (Cambridge: Harvard University Press, 1968) pp. 109–110.
20. Ashby, W. Ross. *Introduction to Cybernetics* (London: Chapman & Hall, 1957) p. 9.
21. Smith, Terry. "Contemporary Art and Contemporaneity" in *Critical Inquiry*, Vol. 32, No. 4 (Summer 2006) p. 688.
22. Betancourt, Michael. "The Aura of the Digital" in *CTheory*, September 5, 2006 http://ctheory.net/articles.aspx?id=519, accessed December 11, 2015.
23. Barker, Tim. "Aesthetics of the Error: Media Art, the Machine, the Unforseen, and the Errant" in *Error: Glitch Noise and Jam in New Media Cultures*, ed. Mark Nunes (New York: Bloomsbury, 2011) pp. 46–48.

1 Origins of "Glitch" in *The Stoppage*

Glitch is not necessarily a new or specifically digital form. Whether in audible or visible media, technical failures have been employed for decades.[1] Engagement with mechanical, automated processes and the (mal)function of machines is a recurring theme of avant-garde art in the twentieth century. However, digital artists are *not* engaged in such basic issues of engineering that they are developing their own custom chips in a fashion equivalent to historical artists such as Thomas Wilfred or Mary Hallock-Greenewalt who invented, then patented novel hardware designs; more like the artist who codes their own software, glitch artists engage the material of digital code through practices that modify existing systems; thus they are idiosyncratic adaptations of current, existing technologies. This history of adaptation describes a range of practices starting before World War II, from Marcel Duchamp's generative music compositions to Jean Tinguely's machine sculptures, and continues with post-war groups such as Experiments in Art and Technology (E.A.T.) and Survival Research Labs in the 1960s and 70s. Digital artists such as Jodi (the artist duo Joan Heemskerk and Dirk Paesmans), Cory Archangel, Brody Condon, or Heath Bunting, as well as all those artists working with video game technology, continue this engagement into the present.

These technical failures have a central place in the general history of film, video and digital imaging. Electronic oscillation patterns, changes to the gamma range, the isolation of object edges and the transformations by signal noise that alter stable video signals are all identified as technical failures in the TV receiver repair handbooks made by RCA in the 1950s;[2] Nam June Paik's video processing recreates these problems for technicians to diagnose and correct when repairing and tuning this equipment. The integration of art and technology that leads directly to visual glitch as a historical artistic practice begins with these specifically visual/music experiments. Analog video processing emerges from technical failures in a premonition of the digital glitching of later decades. This consistent engagement with technical failure reveals an approach that does not assume these "problems" are necessarily negative.

1.1

Contemporary artistic engagement with machinery has taken on a distinct form, most especially evident with the ever-increasing ability of machines to automate what were otherwise cost- and labor-intensive practices. There are three distinct variants in understanding the aesthetic materials generated by machines, and digital systems involve all three approaches—in the computer hardware that executes the code, in the particular creation of the code itself, and finally as the results of that code's being executed on a computer, the results have been conceptualized as

1. proof of concept;
2. vehicle for production;
3. art object in itself.

The issue of the artist's agency in relation to what the machine produces, the digital work, has a recurring significance: this particular heritage begins with the invention of photography, accelerates with electrification (the various music visualizers of the late nineteenth and early twentieth centuries). While there are many artists who code their own software, few digital artists are actively engaged in constructing their hardware in the way that their ancestors in the nineteenth century were. It is the willingness to engage with unanticipated and non-standard outcomes of technical failure that connects the history of digital glitches with this earlier media art.

Contemporary parallels between glitch music and glitch visuals—their use in music parallels their roles in image generation for visual art—emerge simultaneously in Jay Fenton's *Digital TV Dinner* (1978/1979) and other computer videos produced under the rubric of "visual music."[3] These first digital glitches were created in the 1970s by artists in Chicago. The structural limits imposed by visual music on this origin for digital video glitches illuminates the relationship between the early video glitches and later developments. It also anticipates the performative aspects of game art.

Video artists in 1970s Chicago worked with digital software to control a variety of tasks, most famously to automate control over the Sandin Image Processor (IP); however, these developments were not limited to work with Sandin's IP—a variety of applications and roles for digital imaging were being created, including the programming and development of video game systems. Contemporary groups such as Jodi and the variety of glitch artists employing games and interactivity continue this process of investigation;

while they are related, the glitches arising from interactive works are beyond the scope of the present discussion. The particulars of this historical lineage impact the approaches artists have deployed in their development and use of machinery (both physical and immaterial or digital) *in* and *as* their work. The generative potential of digital technology for the production of new imagery and sound moves fluidly between conventional, recognizable forms and noise or technical breakdown.[4] The dynamic created by glitch is a tension between coherence and decoherence increasingly familiar from everyday media.

Digital TV Dinner was initially produced in 1978 by Jamie Fenton and Raul Zaritsky; Dick Ainsworth created the music.[5] It provides a model for the linkage of glitched visuals with their recognizable source, as well as their combination with audio or music. The horizons of expectation associated with glitch video originate not with digital technology but its use within the context of the Chicago video art in the 1970s. It was originally shown at "Electronic Visualization Event #3," a program of visual music video art organized by video artists Dan Sandin and Tom DeFanti's *Electronic Visualization Laboratory* (Chicago, May, 1978).[6] The *EVE* program was prepared in advance and screened in a 500-seat theater using a high-intensity GE video projector.[7] A second version of *Digital TV Dinner* was later broadcast in March 1979 on Episode 11 of the WTTW program *Image Union* that highlighted local video and film.[8]

After being posted online to YouTube in 2009, this video was rapidly adopted by Contemporary glitch artists as an early exemplar of visuals produced under the catch-all name glitch. This video is one of the first to create this type of visual digital glitch and employ it as the primary source material. While this effect was novel in the 1970s, it was anticipated by the use of analog failures in 1960s video art. The extent of this video's embrace and recognition by glitch artists is immediately apparent from its common presence on websites associated with glitch. In spite of this general reposting and mention-citation, there is almost no information, history or discussion of it available beyond the quotation of the YouTube descriptive text; it is prominent enough that it appears in the Wikipedia article on "glitch art,"[9] but even this discussion provides no additional information about the work not already contained by the original 2009 posting on YouTube.com. This rapid embrace-dissemination reveals the close similarity between Fenton's 1978 work and that of Contemporary "glitch" videos as well as the murkiness of this history even as it retains a now-familiar dynamic between recognizable elements and their procedural abstraction by the glitch itself. The early date of this tape, coupled with the approach to creating its visuals (described in an uncredited voice-over attributed to Tom DeFanti) make it one of the first, if not the *very first* glitch video.[10]

Typical for home computer games in the 1970s, the *Bally Astrocade: The Professional Arcade Expandable Computer System* attached to a TV set through its antenna connection, enabling its output to be readily recorded by connecting it to a VTR. The description of the version of *Digital TV Dinner* provided on YouTube provided technical details about its initial production, but not all of the information in this posting is completely accurate:

> *Digital TV Dinner* is a video art clip from 1979 created by Raul Zaritsky, Jamie Fenton, and Dick Ainsworth using the *Bally Astrocade* console game to generate unusual patterns.
>
> The *Bally Astrocade* was unique among cartridge games in that it was designed to allow users to change game cartridges with power-on. When pressing the reset button, it was possible to remove the cartridge from the system and induce various memory dump pattern sequences. Digital TV Dinner is a collection of these curious states of silicon epilepsy set to music composed and generated upon this same platform.
>
> DTV first appeared at an Electronic Visualization Festival in Chicago, and we hear the voice of Dr. Thomas DeFanti introducing this item to the audience.[11]

In an emailed response to an earlier draft of this history, Fenton expanded on the information posted with the YouTube video about the technical details of transferring the *Astrocade* video game systems' output to videotape:

> There were two unique aspects of the *Astrocade* that made *DTVD* possible. First, the video was legal NTSC so it could be recorded. None of the other game consoles was. Second, as you note, you could change cartridges with the power turned on. All of our competitors made you power-down before changing carts.[12]

A standard video (NTSC) output from the *Astrocade* is unusual. The computer game systems available in the 1970s, such as the *Atari 2600 Video Computer System* game console, separated their graphics into entirely different fields for each frame of the video.[13] This meant that each frame showed two different images, making recording them to tape difficult without specialized hardware (such as a time base corrector) to fix these inherent problems with their non-standard NTSC video signal. The use of standard NTSC video as the output for the *Bally Astrocade* meant it was a system uniquely suited for this type of graphic experimentation with its digitally generated output recorded and presented as video art.

The description posted on YouTube implies it is the same as the version shown at the festival; however, this video is not the one included in

Figure 1.1 Typed title card for *Digital TV Dinner* from *EVE3* (1978)

the *Electronic Visualization Event 3 Distribution Tape* from the May 1978 event (the "Electronic Visualization Festival" mentioned in the YouTube description). The differences between these versions are subtle, and do not change the substance of the video itself: the original *Digital TV Dinner* on the *EVE3* tape has only a simple shot of a typed label [Figure 1.1] that provides credits for the piece; there is no voice-over or other explanation of the tape. The version posted on YouTube is *not* this original, first version shown in 1978. It is a variation that adds a voice-over attributed to Tom DeFanti that explains how the video was produced. It also adds two title cards: the first at the head states "Digital TV Dinner Jay Fenton Raul Zaritsky" [Figure 1.2] and an end card stating "Audio by Dick Ainsworth" [Figure 1.3]. The version of *Digital TV Dinner* posted on YouTube in 2009 is identical to the second version of the tape, which was shown in *Image Union* Episode 11, broadcast on March 20, 1979. That the program was from 1979, rather than 1978, makes it a likely source for this digitized version, and accounts for the discrepancy in dating (1978/1979). *Image Union* aired on WTTW, the public television station in Chicago because, unlike similar programs produced to air on "access channels" provided by

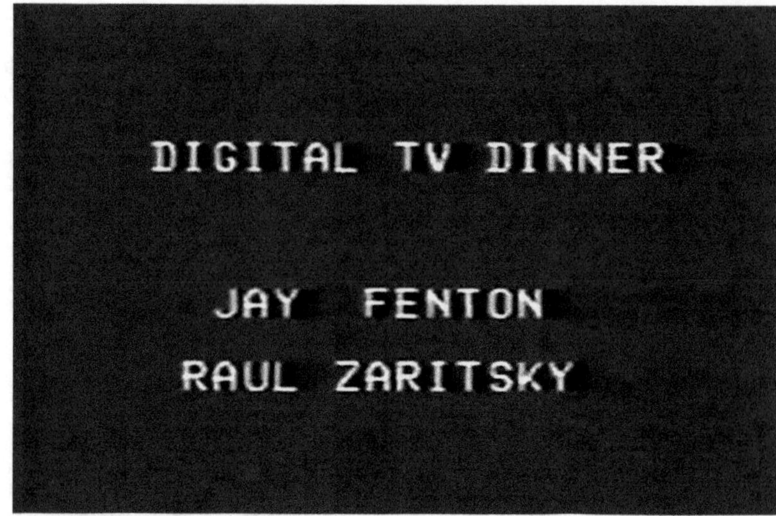

Figure 1.2 Title card for *Digital TV Dinner* from *Image Union,* Episode 11 (1979)

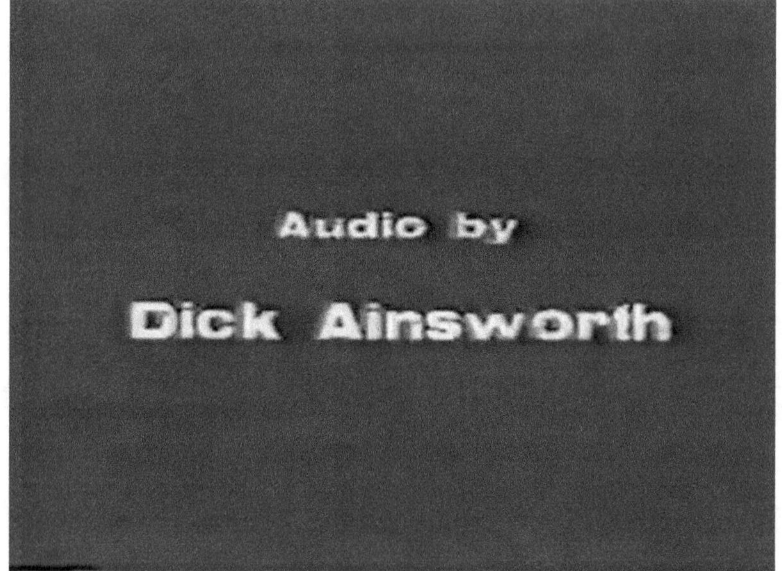

Figure 1.3 "Audio by Dick Ainsworth" title card for *Digital TV Dinner* from *Image Union,* Episode 11 (1979)

CableTV in other cities such as New York where CableTV was introduced in the early 1970s (alongside the introduction of portable video recording equipment), CableTV did not arrive in Chicago until the 1980s.[14] This difference impacted the development of what Michael Shamberg termed "Guerrilla Television" in his book of the same name:

> Guerrilla Television is grassroots television. It works with people, not up from above them. On a simple level, this is no more than "do-it-yourself-TV." But the context for that notion is that survival in an information environment demands information tools.[15]

The opposition to broadcast TV is an explicit part of this approach to media production/distribution, but in the Chicago area, the difficulty of distribution—provided by the cable access channel elsewhere—necessitated a compromise. WTTW's first series featuring independent video productions, *Nightwatch*, hosted by Gene Siskel as a call-in show where the programs were secondary to his celebrity presence, was replaced by *Image Union*. Organized by Tom Weinberg, who was part of the TVTV video collective, it initially drew from his connections with the local video community and work made at the *Chicago Editing Center* that provided access to video production tools.[16] *Image Union* thus reflected the interests and concerns of *Guerrilla Television*, even though it aired on PBS. The program was a 60-minute long anthology of tapes and films produced in the Chicago area, broken into two 30-minute sections. The first half-hour includes motion graphics: TV commercials, logos for industrial companies, as well as student animations and political anti-capitalism cartoons. The diversity of this first half shows a vibrant, dynamic media community where artistic, commercial and scientific interests overlapped in an interdisciplinary fashion. The commonplace distinctions between avant-garde and commercial work are ignored in this selection. The variety of materials on display closely mirrors the mixture of avant-garde and commercial works in the popular-oriented film exhibitions of the 1940s–1960s such as Frank Stauffacher's *Art in Cinema* (1946–54) in San Francisco, or Amos Vogel's *Cinema 16* (1950–63) in New York.[17] *Digital TV Dinner* headlines the second half of the show, what a voice-over on the interstitial credits for *Image Union* describes as "videotapes by Chicago computer image video artists." Both Fenton and Zaritsky were part of the Chicago video art community. This collection of (mostly) abstract videos were all made with digital systems, documenting the relationship between these early digital imaging systems and even earlier analog video.

Digital TV Dinner is the first of a series of videos in this episode made by Fenton; in fact, all of the computer videos except one (*Electronic Boogie* by Bob Snyder) credit Fenton as either the lead artist or as collaborator.

Image Union, Episode 11 documents the historical shift emerging from the introduction of the microcomputer in 1974. All the digital videos in this episode were produced with *home* computers—unlike computer films from earlier in the 1970s by Stan VanDerBeek or Lillian Schwartz at Bell Labs and John Whitney at IBM; Sandin and DeFanti's own use of the PDP-11 to control the IP are all examples of computer-generated works which were much more difficult to produce, and consequently required corporate or institutional support. However, even in context with a number of other computer works by Fenton, *Digital TV Dinner* is unusual: it is almost entirely unlike the next video, *Grafix* by Fenton, Nola Donato and Tom DeFanti, which demos a software designed to use the Bally home computer game hardware. The flat geometric forms appearing during the title and introductory voice-over in the *Grafix* demo tape that follows *Digital TV Dinner* in the *Image Union* program demonstrates their similarity to the other graphics the *Astrocade* would generate when operating normally; it shows "paint" software created for the *Astrocade* game console. The relationship between the visuals created by the (art) *Digital TV Dinner* tape and this documentary tape is only apparent in the expressive graphics appearing at the start for the *Grafix* title, rather than the less dynamic, instructional footage showing both the software code and what it looks then when in use. While the title card for *Grafix* is abstract [Figure 1.4]

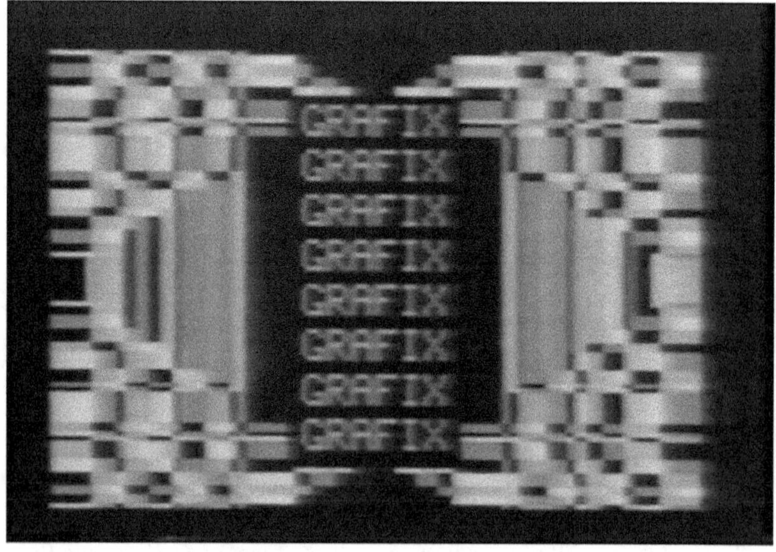

Figure 1.4 Title card for *Grafix* from *Image Union*, Episode 11 (1979)

and presents highly graphic geometric forms in motion, the rest of the video is more typical of consumer "computer art" systems being created in the late 1970s and early 1980s, demonstrating several simple art programs: one for painting, another for music, including showing how easy it is to code for them. The educational potentials of this software are the focus of the *Grafix* video, not its use to create art.

Digital TV Dinner is *not* a use of software—it is an exploit of technical failure. The imagery appearing in this video is *not* designed. Instead, it emerges spontaneously as the processor memory faults when the game cartridge is prematurely removed from the console. These images are a result of the digital processor glitching *after* the program being run is unexpectedly interrupted. *Digital TV Dinner* is the only video shown that was not made by writing a program specifically to generate its imagery, a fact that is immediately obvious in context with these other computer videos.

1.2

The *Electronic Visualization Laboratory* founded in 1973 at the University of Illinois at Chicago was devoted to interdisciplinary work—specifically the exploration and development of computer imaging as it intersected with video art.[18] The *Electronic Visualization Event 3 Distribution Tape* that includes the first version of *Digital TV Dinner* runs 60 minutes and contains a variety of video works; however, even though the approaches and techniques on display are quite disparate, the videos are all examples of the "visual music" genre of video art. Of the eight videos in the collection, *Digital TV Dinner* is the only work where either Fenton or Zaritsky is credited. In reviewing this "distribution tape," their digital video is clearly produced using a technique unlike anything else on the tape—even though some of the other pieces do resemble computer art, *Digital TV Dinner* is utterly unlike them in its imagery, even as it is recognizably a work of visual music. These differences make the piece seem anomalous in context with other video art productions from *Electronic Visualization Event 3*, all of which have a similar aesthetic of kinetic forms suspended in a black space; several of them employ signal processing suggesting their creation involved using Sandin's IP.

The visual music (synaesthetic) tradition is determinant of the form assumed not only by *Digital TV Dinner*, but all the works curated in the *EVE3* screening. It is a typical example of the "Chicago school" of video in the 1970s, where the tapes are simultaneously formal demonstrations of new techniques, and organized musically in ways that develop from the earlier history of visual music film animation. Sheldon Brown, Director of the Center for Research in Computing and the Arts at the University of

California, San Diego described these experiments in his introduction to a survey exhibition of Sandin and DeFanti's collaborations in 2011:

> This work has more in common with some threads of avant-garde conversations in art film deriving from poetry and painting than it did with emerging video art growing from conceptual art, performance art and cultural theory. The work of Sandin and collaborators could occasionally be heard characterized as "video wallpaper," but its reach was already influential to other pioneering figures such as Nam June Paik and the Vasulkas.[19]

Those threads of avant-garde film Brown describes are visible as the history of abstract or *absolute* film, that genre of production also known as visual music. These works tended to be oriented towards visual forms that suggested hallucinatory states and synaesthesia[20]; the history of synaesthetic avant-garde film and video converges on the history of abstract painting in form, meaning and aspiration. Apparent links between an early work such as *Digital TV Dinner* and later visual music performances such as *VJ* may be less an explicit historical influence of this particular video, than the structural influence and limiting conditions produced by the emphasis on creating performative synaesthesia common to visual music generally and the tradition as a whole. (Both Wilfred and Hallock-Greenewalt's visual music machines, created by 1920, were designed for live performance.) The importance of this early work with digital glitches is principally anticipatory: it provides an explicit connection between Contemporary developments with digital glitches and the earlier innovations of analog video processing, while at the same time connecting their form and meaning to an earlier tradition of synaesthetic-optical experiments with film such as Norman McLaren's *Synchromy* (1971), Oskar Fischinger's *Ornament Sound* (1932) or Rudolf Pfenninger's *Tones from Out of Nowhere* (1931) all of which employ highly graphic, repeating imagery[21] resembling the glitch imagery in *Digital TV Dinner*.

The synaesthetic visual tradition of visual art becomes a structural determinant of the form and reception of visual music in *EVE3.* Hallucinatory states provided inspiration and a direct referent for the synaesthetic imagery used by some of these artists; Fenton, in an email exchange, explained her inspiration for *Digital TV Dinner* in precisely these *psychedelic* terms:

> One weekend I was tripping on a drug called ALD-52 (which is like LSD), with some friends. At dinner time, I was playing around with the *Bally Arcade* by popping out the cartridge during the boot-up sequence and saw the machine go into a particularly complex glitch animation

> sequence. It occurred to me that the machine was "tripping" just like I was. Later, with a video recorder connected, I tried to recreate that experience. I was never able to get it into the extended animation that I saw earlier. Instead we cut together several glitches into the tape we later showed at the festival.
>
> So glitches begat glitches and dinner begat dinner.[22]
>
> [. . .]
>
> Raul and Dick were not partying with me when I "discovered" *DTVD.* Raul did the video editing and Dick did the sound track. Dick wrote the manual for a program I created called "Bally Basic," which for a few months held the title of "cheapest computer you could program yourself."[23]

The relationship Fenton describes between a personal, subjective experience and the formal organization of imagery in the finished work is a common part of the visual music tradition's heritage. This subjectivist dimension also found application in the kinds of transformations Sandin's IP could produce—both as an analog machine, and as an analog-digital hybrid (by the mid-1970s, Sandin and DeFanti employed a PDP-11 computer for precise control of its effects[24]). The morphology and structure of audio-visual glitches in *Digital TV Dinner* reflects the contextual demand of synaesthetic media (visual music) common to Chicago video art. Its history provides a clear understanding of what glitch means in a visual art context, and establishes the scope of this term—and the technical failures it identifies—in Contemporary digital video practice: later glitch art recapitulates these earlier developments.

It exploits machinic *mis*function that is potential in any digital video system: understanding the technology remains a constant element of glitches generally, whether visual or audible. Fenton was deeply familiar with the mechanical nature of this process and its degrees of freedom because she was the programmer writing games for the *Astrocade* at the company where she worked:

> There was ROM memory in the cartridge and ROM memory built into the console. Popping out the cartridge while executing code in the console ROM created garbage references in the stack frames and invalid pointers, which caused the strange patterns to be drawn.[25]

The organization of the strange patterns these glitches produced is through the conventions of visual music, rendering them coherent within the 1970s Chicago video art scene. The idea of visual music acts to organize the form and direct the interpretation of the work for audiences familiar with its codes; these historical protocols organize the digital materiality visualized on screen. Her implicit, thorough knowledge of the *Astrocade* hardware and software, coupled with the specific context of its premiere at *Electronic Visualization Event 3,* makes this early use of digital glitches less surprising.

The serial graphics so readily apparent in *Digital TV Dinner* have remained a common, formal feature of glitch video: repeating flat graphics, both within individual shots and across the range of shots in the whole video, are typical of Contemporary visual glitches produced as both still images and video. The fusion of recognizable content—fragmentary, identifiable menu text and other graphics from the game system—with complex, anticipates later works with glitch where repetitive abstract patterns contain recognizable elements becoming increasingly abstract, recalling the same forms as in Iman Moradi's *Gltch Aesthetics*: fragmentation, replication/repetition and linearity [Figure 1.5].[26] All of these structures appear in the failures recorded and used in *Digital TV Dinner*. The graphic character of these glitches converges on later interventions in *re*programming code within the computer system itself. The distinct features of glitch are associated with serial structures, suggesting autonomously looping computer code generating a result and then repeating/iterating it as a series of similar patterns across the screen. The varieties of generative imagery appearing in Fenton's video recur in later glitch work by artists such as Ant Scott, and are abundantly on view in *Glitch: Designing Imperfection*, a book that collects in still form the visual work of many glitch artists. Moradi explains the procedures generating this imagery in his introduction:

> For the glitch artists, the process of creating visuals is an involved process, which stems from an understanding of their tools: computer hardware (storage media, memory and display technology) and software (operating systems, imager processing libraries, file storage and data transmission protocols). Fundamentally though, everything boils down to principles of composition, color and personal taste, which are immutably non-specific and timeless. Aesthetic considerations therefore govern the way glitch artists crop, compose and even provoke the generation of these images.[27]

The structural limits imposed by aesthetic considerations link these works to the history of art and introduce the artist's role as editor into the selection/creation of the work as a variety of "found footage" that connects glitch to other forms of appropriate and collage in art. At the same time, the heritage of Constructivist abstraction is equally apparent in the repeating, serial graphic forms generated by the digital computer; the convergence between the formal, graphic organization of early computer graphics and historical

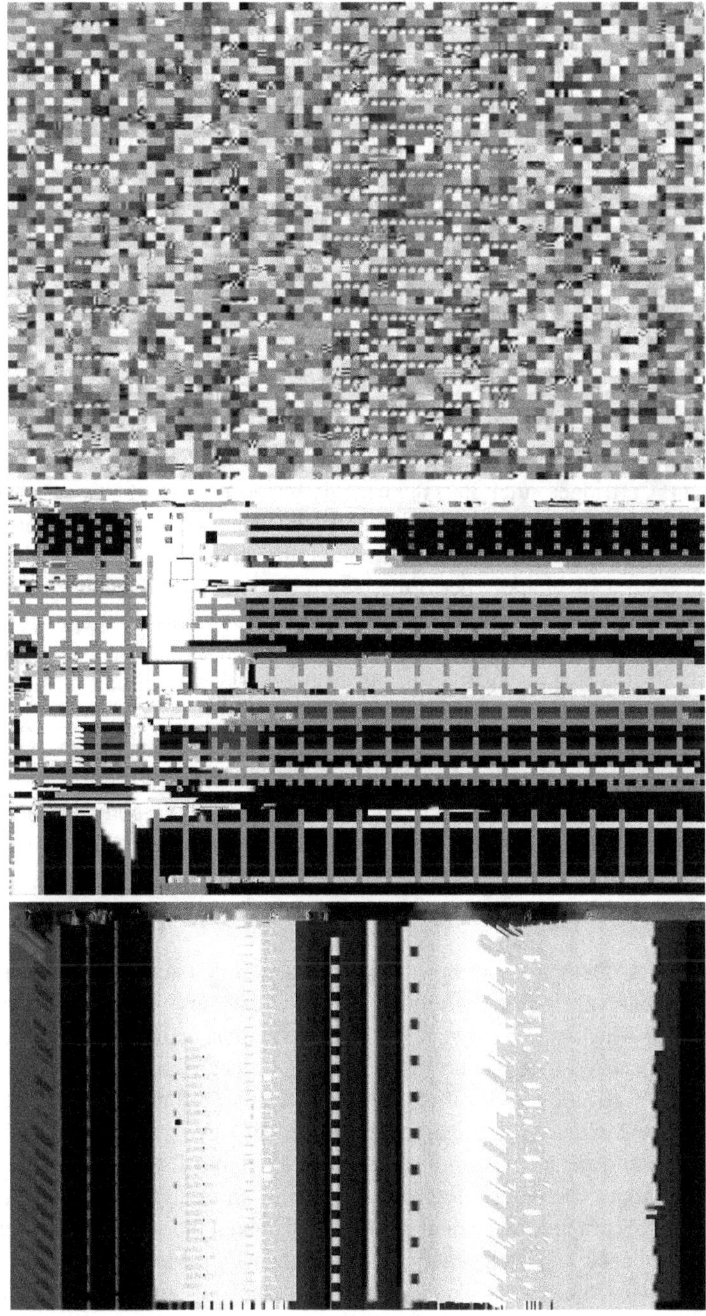

Figure 1.5 Repeating graphic elements characteristic of visual glitches

abstract painting was noted by the 1970s by pioneering computer artists such as Lillian Schwartz.[28] The imagery in *Digital TV Dinner* resembles Josef Alber's pictures composed from bands and blocks of color, forms that are themselves similar and convergent with the colored synaesthetic bands in McLaren's *Synchromy.* The visual music tradition's concerns with the technological creation of audible sound as a visual form have an analogous morphology to these visuals generated digitally, even though the innate connection between sound and image in these films is absent from *Digital TV Dinner* due to the technological differences between optical sound and digital software.

1.3

Digital TV Dinner was created with an exploit of the *Bally Astrocade* game system. Cartridges stuck into the console would pop out if you struck the case, creating anomalous digital imagery; the video included an experimental music track created with a variation on this same exploit. These glitches result from a specifically performative process that Tom DeFanti explains in voice over during the credits (he is uncredited on the tape) opening the *Image Union* version from 1979, and continuing into the start of the video itself, making this explanation of the production process a part of the tape itself, he states:

> This piece represents the absolute cheapest one can go in home computer art. This involves taking a $300 video game system, pounding it with your fist so the cartridge pops out while it's trying to write the menu.
>
> The music here is done by Dick Ainsworth using the same system, but pounding it with your fingers instead of your fist.

The process DeFanti describes for the creation of this audio-visual work is one that emphasizes the performative over (and against) the explicitly programmed. The focus on a dynamic, subjective human action was common to artists associated with Sandin and DeFanti in Chicago during the 1970s: the idea of "electronic visualization" was specifically performative—an active engagement with analog and digital media technology—rather than passive, an image to watch,[29] making Fenton's adaptation of it for use with the new, cheaper home computer a logical extension of an established approach. It necessarily contains an element of uncertainty about the result, even though an experienced and well-practiced performer would likely know approximately what the results would be: these images are an interruption in a technical protocol that is entirely predictable in a strictly determinate fashion, even if in practice, the results are less so. The simultaneously limited degrees of freedom for the *Astrocade* and the ability to mechanical iterate (thus exhaust) this range of potentials produces iterative completeness based in the granular (pixelated) data that is a fundamental condition of digitality.

In *Digital TV Dinner* the generation of imagery by a performance glitch depends on when the human actor causes a stoppage of the autonomous process; the result is "unanticipated imagery." These transformations have become a standard part of the visual language of media art generally, a structural determinant of interpretation as Brown notes:

> Bit-depth, gamma range, object edges and noise were some of the new compositional elements that analog and digital signal processing made apparent. Over the following decades this new semantics permeated image culture at large, becoming the *de facto* material basis by which media is produced.[30]

Brown's analysis suggests the transformative effect of Sandin's IP on analog video can be understood in a *materialist* sense: that the electronic video signal is the "real" video, its display simply a translation of those encoded instructions into tangible form shown on a monitor/TV, or via projection. Glitch offers electronic and digital systems a direct parallel to earlier avant-garde film techniques such as scratching the film stock, direct animations that hand-paint their imagery without a camera, or photogram and collage techniques—such as in Man Ray's *Retour à la raisonne* (1923), or Stan Brakhage's *Moth Light* (1961) made without photography. These "materialist" engagements with celluloid are prominently linked to glitch in Kathryn Ramey's textbook of physical film techniques, *Experimental Filmmaking*; glitch is the only digital procedure she addresses:

> There is a sense of continuity between film artists such as JJ Murphy and his most well known work *Print Generation* and the work of artists such as Christophe Behrens and Will Hurt (glitchCORD) who repeated digital compression or the compression that results from putting images through several different transfer processes (uploading, downloading, copying to VHS, etc.).[31]

The continuity between these earlier film engagements with the celluloid as a physical material/reproductive technology and the Contemporary deployment of glitches along similar conceptual lines unites the digital work with earlier films. However, the technical difference is significant: where the material degradation common to film rephotography and printing and the data loss of compression that Ramey identifies provide a parallel to the generative and procedural nature of digital media that nevertheless forcibly separates these image technologies; visual glitches result from stoppage—the interruption of a predictable and prescribed autonomous process.

Glitch is thus analogous to earlier materialist approaches to motion imaging employed by both avant-garde film and video art. The disintegration of motion imagery in Takeshi Murata's digital videos follow this same pattern: a recognizable image is repeatedly transformed by a glitch process called "datamoshing" that renders its initially familiar forms as progressively more unstable and abstract graphics. The progressions in Murata's *Monster Movie* (2005) shift between recognizable imagery of the "yeti" from the 1981 film *Caveman* (a monster that evokes earlier B-movies) that becomes abstract fields of moving color [Figure 1.6] through the manipulation of the digital file itself: datamoshing removes image data from the mpeg compressed video, resulting in the characteristic smears and abstraction apparent in this video. The stoppages inherent to this process reveal a digital failure resulting from the unintelligent mechanical protocol proceeding normally. The imagery appearing on screen reflects a stoppage of this typically proceeding sequence—creating visuals that reflect a partial implementation of the instructions contained by the digital code. For Adorno, this momentary rupture has the capacity to shock its audience into realizing how artificial the apparent unity of the work is.[32]

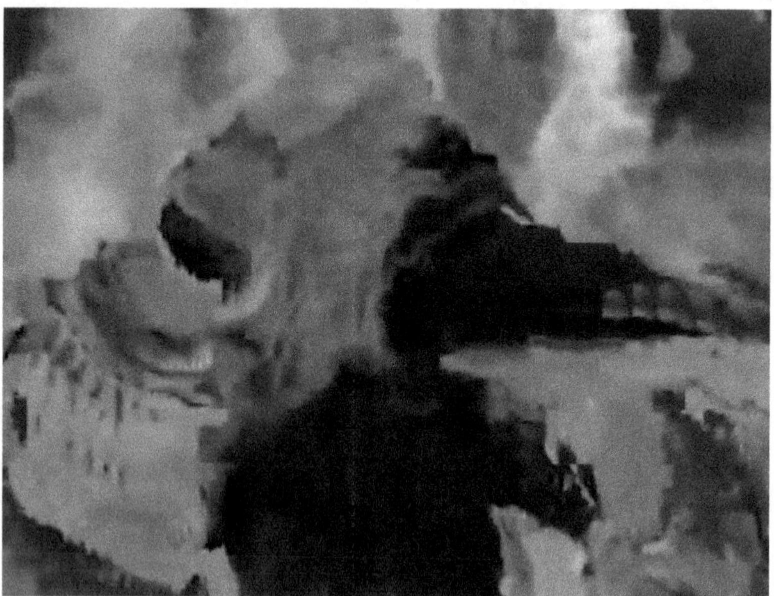

Figure 1.6 Still from *Monster Movie* (2005), by Takeshi Murata

1.4

Digital glitching is a purely deterministic process: each interruption at the same point will produce identical results—these constants are the *mechanical* nature of the generated imagery, a function of its limited degrees of freedom. In practice causing a stoppage at *exactly* the same instant in the code's execution is problematic, giving the results their unanticipated-yet-predictable character as the mechanical processing of the code is entirely constrained in advance. The system already contains all the glitch imagery as potential results of the deterministic, iterative completeness fundamental to digital production. Marcel Duchamp's musical compositions are a paradigmatic example of how the avant-garde has historically exploited iterative completeness. The importance of the iterations does not lie within the mechanically described range, but rather with the interpretative interventions of the artistic consciousness; these interventions are the same stoppages[33] imposed by the performative element of *Digital TV Dinner.*

What appears on screen has a physical origin, it is not an execution of code, but the interruption in that code's execution—a stoppage—that creates the glitch: while the imagery is serially structured in a repeating fashion—simple blocks of graphics repeat across the screen, and the anomalous visuals *do* have a recurring graphic form—the imagery that does appear cannot be predicted or controlled with the same precision that graphics specifically generated by code. This performance-aspect shifts what appears from the realm of programming executed automatically, to the particular touch of the individual handling the machine. It seems to open the autonomous protocols of the machine, controlled in advance by the strictures of the code, to the vagaries of human interaction. The violence—"beating it with your fist"—that provides this interruption is at the same time a performance/intervention that breaks the normative flow of processes and autonomous actions, a human-determined stoppage that redirects the machine.

That the same technique can produce both the visuals (banging the case with a fist) and sounds (tapping the same case with fingers) heard in *Digital TV Dinner* is an indication of how touch-sensitive this type of glitch-manipulation can be. Thus, the results are utterly predictable, without being fully prescriptive of the result. This balance between predictability and a chaotic, unknown result is a common feature of the stoppage employed in creating glitches, uniting what happens in this video with more recent developments.

Individual "shots" (stoppages) have a high degree of self-similarity, but are nevertheless distinguishable as unique instances of the same underlying glitch technique applied to the same sequence of instructions. This idea of "stoppage" originates with Marcel Duchamp's work *La Mariée mise à nu par ses célibataires même. Erratum Musicale,* as composer Peter Kotik explains about his work realizing it for performance in 1987:

> The apparatus composing the piece is comprised of three parts: a funnel, several open top cars, and a set of numbered balls. . . . The placing of notes (numbers) in the score was determined by the way in which the balls came through the funnel and were taken out of the cars. . . . The composition itself was determined by Duchamp in his description of the system and his examples of musical scoring.[34]

The score for Duchamp's composition is the product of instructions writing in 1912–1913. The precise sequence of notes to be played are "chosen" by a mechanical process. The problems with this score arise not from the machine, but the incompleteness of its result: even though these works are technically deterministic—limited set of elements, limited set of possible outcomes (all possible arrangements of notes in the score could be worked out mathematically as a permutation set). The score has the character of being random because there is no over-riding human intelligence selecting a particular order; where each individual score or implementation is a particular instance of an autonomous machine function, yet (paradoxically) is deflected from being purely mechanical through the intervention of an interpreting consciousness; different assumptions made about how to resolve the stoppages necessarily would produce a different score. The dialectic between defined (instructions) and undefined (interpretation/"desire of interpreter") appears to generate a limiting framework with clearly delineated degrees of freedom; however, this system is undermined at its foundation by the interpreter who must "fill in" details to follow Duchamp's instructions *as written.* The machine function is interrupted by the human choice, the resulting delay creates the stoppage. They are breakdowns where the mechanical process stops, literally invisible in his score (until Kotik attempted to generate it following Duchamp's protocol), these stoppages become immanently visible with digital video as the interrupted function of the machine dumping its data buffer to the video monitor/display. This distinction between Duchamp's (analogue) stoppage and the (digital) stoppage renders the machinic process a material for manipulation and direction.

Fenton's manipulations of the digital computer as an instrumental performance are akin to music, and like music, are dependent on the virtuosity of the performer—for the same reasons. *Digital TV Dinner* participates and reflects this very specific conceptual and aesthetic context both in its form—it is a visualized performance—and in the meaning those forms have as visual accompaniment to the music (as a work of video art in a visual music mode). The machine stops, awaiting further interpretation before proceeding.

All the imagery of *Digital TV Dinner* is composed from *partial* failures: the system breaks, but only so much that the standard, anticipated result does not (entirely) dis/appear. Instead of rebooting, the machine generates visuals following the partial instructions still in memory, dumping the results as the chaotic (but structured) noise shown in the finished video. Glitch as a whole, whether audible or visual, depends on this catastrophic, yet incomplete, breakdown. This process repeats for each shot with slight variations in results that reflect differences in timing: the images created by this process are highly sensitive to what point in the generation of the system menu has been interrupted. The final stoppage that ends the video, by posing as a return to normalcy, forces a recognition that these glitches are precisely a controlled, human choice—challenging the automation of procedures inherent to digital technologies, a recognition that it depends on the human role becoming a conscious acknowledgement by the audience.

The images in *Digital TV Dinner* are quotations, their presence is an acknowledgement of the performative aspects not only of its games, but the actions required to produce these broken graphics and music seen and heard throughout the video: what has been recorded and used in *Digital TV Dinner* is the result of the system *partially* crashing. This video is a document of someone physically manipulating the machinery itself where the system dumps the material in memory on screen as kinetic geometric patterns that move both up and down on screen at different rates. The text appearing at the top of the screen "SELECT GAME" at the beginning [Figure 1.7]

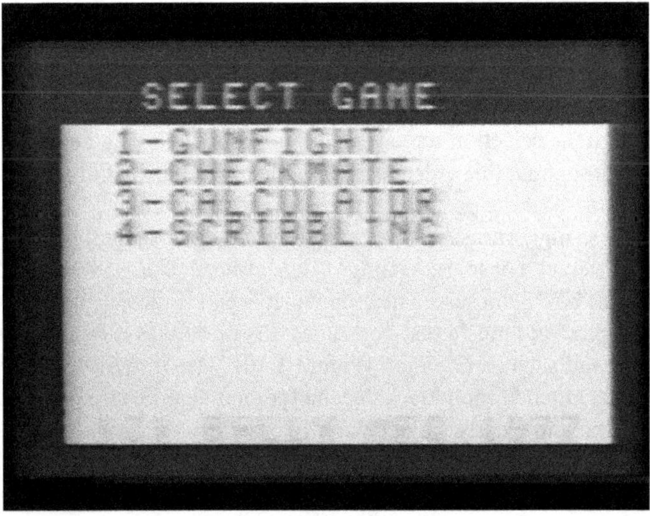

Figure 1.7 Menu from the *Bally Astrocade* appearing in *Digital TV Dinner* (1978)

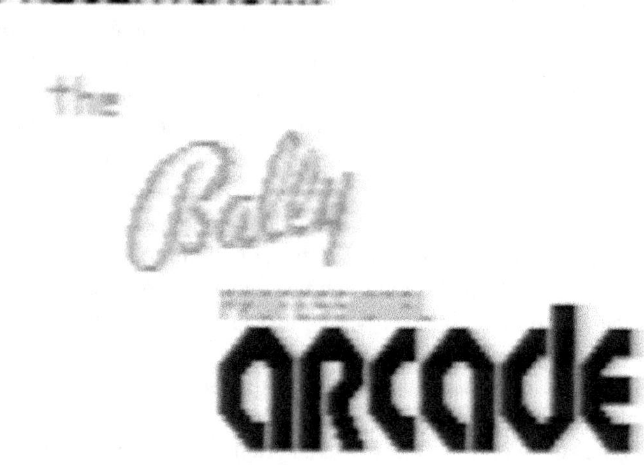

Figure 1.8 Boot screen logos for the *Bally Astrocade* appearing in *Digital TV Dinner* (1978)

reappears sporadically throughout the whole video. Occasionally a partial boot-screen graphic will appear, showing that the interruption is always on the verge of full system failure [Figure 1.8]. It shows at what point the processes generating the screen have been interrupted: this effect is possible in the Bally system because, as Fenton notes, it was one of the only video game systems where cartridges could be removed from the machine without causing a total system crash.

Although the selection screen (menu) appears in varying degrees of dissolution throughout this video, it is possible to read the list of games available on some of these occasionally legible, nearly unglitched screens. This list changes, suggesting the tape is made from either several cartridges, or several different consoles: *Gunfight, Checkmate, Calculator* and *Scribbling* are all briefly on screen near the video's end [Figure 1.9]. The "Game Over" graphic and music that concludes this piece was used by games on the *Astrocade* such as *Gunfight* [Figure 1.10]. The "samples" that can be heard in the glitched soundtrack depend for their significance on being both recognizable and clearly fragmentary, like the legible menu graphics they are found footage directing attention to the normal function of the system. This dynamic of recognition overlaid with misrecognition is a recurring element in both the visual and audible glitch: it renders these glitched elements quotational. The ability to identify sources (or at least the originary subject)

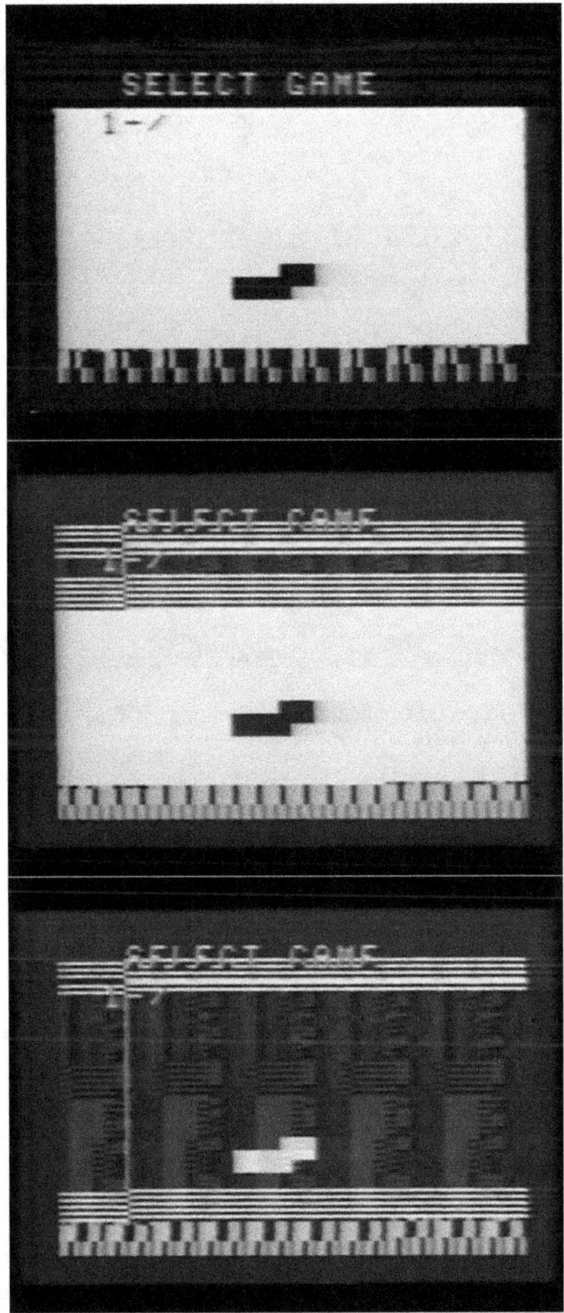

Figure 1.9 Stills from *Digital TV Dinner* (1978) showing "Select Game" text

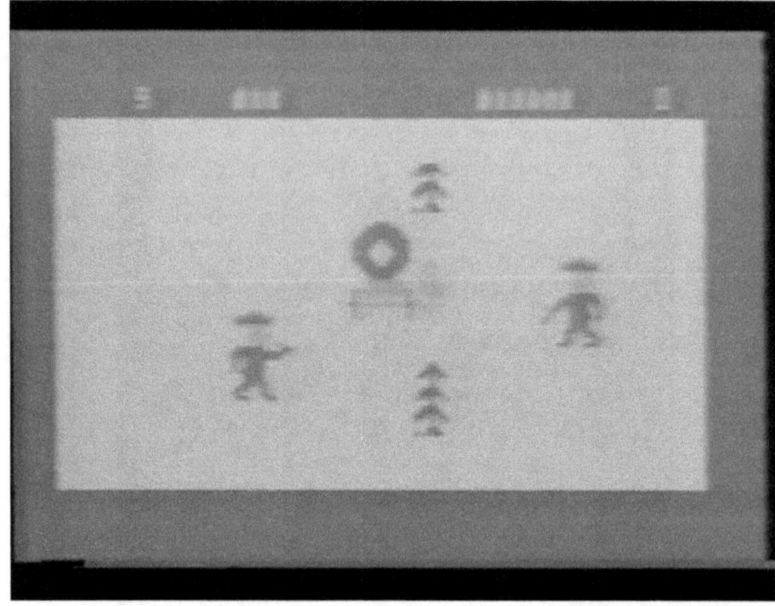

Figure 1.10 Still from the "Gunfight" game appearing in *Grafix* from *Image Union*, Episode 11 (1979)

as well as the decomposition of that source into the formal elements of its digital construction is integral to the organization of *Digital TV Dinner* as a whole. It is the feature that closely links this work to Contemporary glitched works in a way that does not depend on the formal organization of the imagery itself, but rather on the semiotic processes of assembly, transformation and recognition specific to digital sampling in general.

An offhand comment during the *Grafix* documentary about the *Astrocade* defaulting to the video game "*Gunfight*" when it reboots after crashing illuminates the final glitched image showing "GAME OVER" at the end of *Digital TV Dinner* [Figure 1.11]. It is possible this image reflects such a system reboot into the game, rather than into the game selection menu, although selecting a game and then glitching it could produce the same imagery. While it is unclear if any of the other imagery shown is also from a game, the tape does contain images that are produced from the glitched boot screen, making more sources than just the menu screen very likely. When there is a total crash, the machine must reboot—there is no imagery drawn on screen. Rather than producing a procession of strange, repeating patterns,

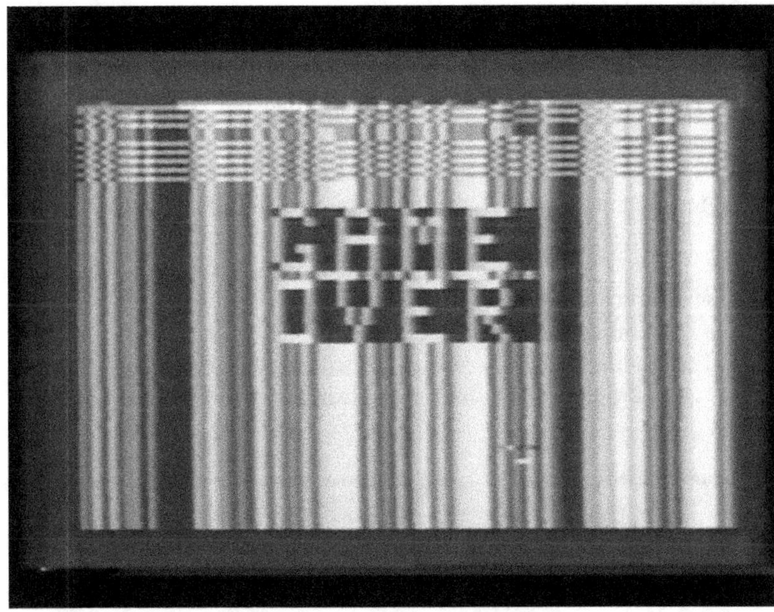

Figure 1.11 "Game Over" text from *Digital TV Dinner* (1978)

the glitched version of the "GAME OVER" text/screen plays the "you're dead" music in a humorous *finalé* where it is the computer game that died, rather than the player. This concluding glitch is an appropriate end to the video—a comic acknowledgement that when glitches distort and transform the computer screen, they are the "death" of normal function: rebooting will be necessary to start over. Evidence of this necessity is scattered throughout the video.

If this concluding eruption of recognizable forms and music are not taken only as a comic ending, but as a comment on the normative function of digital media reasserting itself, in the shift from glitched to non-glitched materials this conclusion presents a stoppage that changes from being governed by the aesthetics of visual music to one that critically challenges the organization and aesthetic structure of the work itself. The "death" of the machine, while funny, is also a revelation of a second integral disruption—a glitching of the glitched visuals themselves. This return to normalcy appears as a violation of the "rules" established by the visual music/glitch throughout the rest of *Digital TV Dinner*, forcing a sudden awareness of the stoppages producing this work as violations of the normal, anticipated function *and* as a violation of the aesthetic transformation these failures have when organized by the structures of visual music.

The insertion of human decisions at crucial points (the stoppage) in an otherwise autonomous process undermines the independent function of the system in question. A breach in normal function, however visible to the audience, is at the same time *not* a failure of the digital system. System failure is *invisible,* it becomes apparent not through *mis*function, but as *mal*function, a cessation—the digital renders *nothing* [Figure 1.12a–c]. *Apparent* imagery of the type the *Astrocade* generates in *Digital TV Dinner* reveals the stoppage imposed by human action has redirected the results of autonomous production; this immanent redirection is identical to what happens in Duchamp's instructions for the composition of *La Mariée mise à nu par ses célibataires même. Erratum Musicale.* For a digital system, the stoppage creates a rupture that becomes visible as the glitch itself. The potential

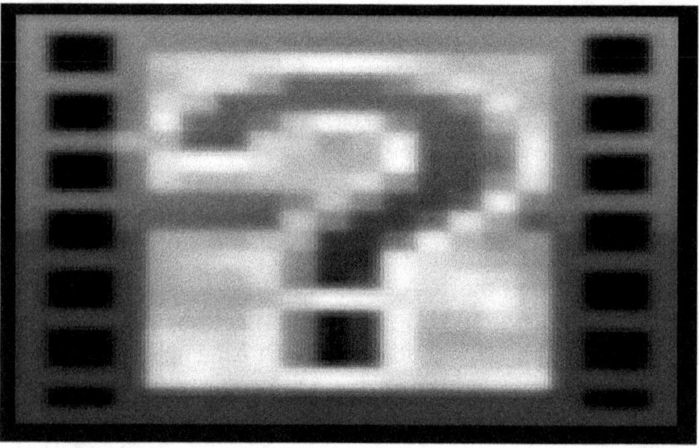

Figure 1.12a Error message: "Unplayable video file"

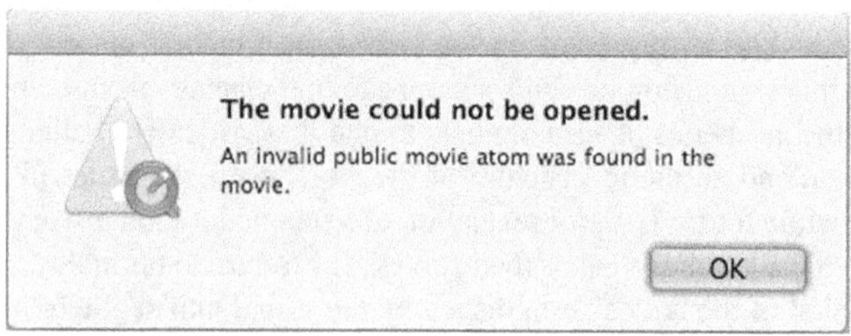

Figure 1.12b Error message: "The movie could not be opened"

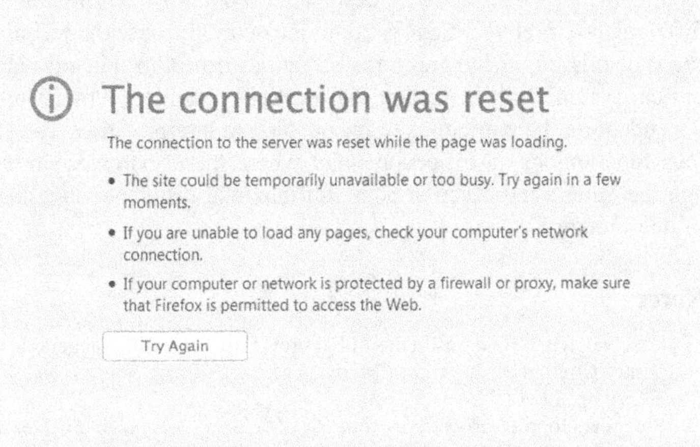

Figure 1.12c Error message: "The connection was reset"

for these stoppages to become vehicles for critical interpretation depends on their relationship to the audience's perception of them as demonstrative not of a *mal*function that can be ignored, but as a *mis*function demanding attention: that is, as a stoppage awaiting human interpretation—even if that interpretation is to dismiss it from consideration following the aura of the digital.

Duchamp's protocol (the autonomous process and stoppage) suggests the need to separate generation from reception—even though that separation is rhetorical rather than immanent as in Kotik's performance of the score. The mechanical nature of Duchamp's process is different by degree only from the autonomous processes of computer graphics being employed in *Digital TV Dinner*. The digital imagery being employed in this glitch video demonstrate their foundation in a stoppage of the *Astrocade* graphics system through even a cursory comparison to other graphics produced with the same system that as the coded, expected results of normal operation. This stoppage offers a potential for critical rupture through its transfiguration of the commonplace elements of the imagery being glitched, but this change is complicated by immanent recognition that the system is broken (an identification that elides any critical potential).

The turn away from critical engagement into the prosaic designation "broken" follows from the resilient nature of digital ideology and capitalism to establish the horizons of interpretation in advance of their challenge, effectively countering critical potentials *before* they emerge. Instead of an acknowledgement of the glitch as rupture, the aura of the digital elides it from consideration—in being designated broken or identified as glitched different interpretive valences come into play. In one, the technical failure is dismissed, its integral transformations neutralized in advance of any critical potential; in the other, their critical potentials remain immanent, dependent on the particulars of encounter and interpretation. The stoppage thus functions as an inflection point where these extremes—one critical and the other not—describe points of maximal difference in a continuum of interpretations.

Notes

1. Cascone, Kim. "The Aesthetics of Failure: 'Post-Digital' Tendencies in Contemporary Computer Music" in *Computer Music Journal*, Vol. 24, No. 4 (Winter, 2000), pp. 12–18.
2. Meagher, John R. *RCA Television Pict-O-Guide: An Aid to TV Troubleshooting, Volume 1* (Harrison, NJ: Radio Corporation of America, Tube Department, 1949), see pp. 45, 49, 51, and 55 for examples of analog signal and technical glitches that reproduce visual phenomena resembling analog signal processing in early video art.
3. Kahn, Douglas. *Noise Water Meat: A History of Sound in the Arts* (Cambridge: MIT Press, 1999).
4. Cascone, Kim. "The Aesthetics of Failure: 'Post-Digital' Tendencies in Contemporary Computer Music" in *Computer Music Journal*, Vol. 24, No. 4 (Winter, 2000) pp. 12–13.
5. *Digital TV Dinner*'s YouTube posting had 3,645 views, and 76 "thumbs-up" approvals by February 4, 2014.
6. It appears in the middle of a program of eight videos: *Wire Trees with 4 Vectors* (video: Phil Morton, Guenther Tetz, audio: Lief Brush, Stu Pettigrew); *By the Crimson Bands of Cyttorak* (video: Tom DeFanti, Barbara Sykes, audio: Glen Charvat, Doug Lofstrom, Rick Panzer, Jim Teister); *Electronic Masks* (video: Barbara Sykes, audio: Glen Charvat, Doug Lofstrom, Tom Warzecha); *Spiral 3* (video: Tom DeFanti, Phil Morton, Dan Sandin, Jane Veeder, dance: Rylin Harris, audio: Sticks Raboin, Bob Snyder); *Digital TV Dinner* (video: Jay Fenton, Raul Zaritsky, audio: Dick Ainsworth); *Data Bursts in 3 Moves* (video Phil Morton, Guenther Tetz, audio Phil Morton, Bob Snyder); *Cetacean* (video: Chip Dodsworth, Phil Morton, audio: Barry Brosch, Chip Dodsworth); *Not of This Earth* (video: Barbra Latham, John Manning, Ed Rankus, audio: Patti Smith). Listed in Stone, Trish. *Synthesis: Processing and Collaboration* (San Diego: The Gallery@Calit2, 2011), p. 42.
7. Fox, Tiffany. "Interview with Dan Sandin and Tom DeFanti" in *Synthesis: Processing and Collaboration* (San Diego: The Gallery@Calit2, 2011) p. 13.
8. It appears in the second half of *Episode 11: Animation*, starting at timecode 36:36. This original broadcast includes the same voice-over at the start as the version posted to YouTube. The video is available in the Media Burn archive: http://mediaburn.org/video/image-union-animation-episode-10/, accessed February 4, 2014.

9. The text summarized what appeared with the YouTube video: "Early examples of glitches used in media art include *Digital TV Dinner* (1979) created by Raul Zaritsky, Jamie Fenton, and Dick Ainsworth by manipulating the Bally video game console and recording the results on videotape." https://en.wikipedia.org/wiki/Glitch_art, accessed February 4, 2014.
10. In a private email discussion with Jamie Fenton on February 7, 2014 she notes about the origins of glitches: "The first 'glitch art' was seen occasionally when we debugged games in 1975. A game crash would spread 'mung,' (or garbage) on the screen. Sometimes the mung had a regularity to it."
11. The second version and its description were uploaded to YouTube on October 8, 2009: http://www.youtube.com/watch?v=Ad9zdlaRvdM, accessed February 4, 2014.
12. Private email discussing this essay prior to publication with Jamie Fenton, February 6, 2014.
13. *Atari 2600 Video Computer System Field Service Manual 2600/2600A Domestic (M/N) FD100133, Rev. 02* (Sunnyvale, CA: Atari, Inc., 1983).
14. Chapman, Sara. "Guerrilla Television in the Digital Age" in *Journal of Film and Video*, Vol. 64, Nos. 1–2 (Spring/Summer, 2012) p. 44.
15. Shamberg, Michael and Raindance Corporation. "Manual" in *Guerrilla Television* (New York: Holt, 1971) p. 8. The book is composed of two sections, "Meta-Manual" and "Manual," each numbered separately.
16. Chapman, Sara. "Guerrilla Television in the Digital Age" in *Journal of Film and Video*, Vol. 64, Nos. 1–2 (Spring/Summer, 2012) p. 46.
17. MacDonald, Scott. *Art in Cinema: Documents towards a History of the Film Society* (Philadelphia: Temple University Press, 2010).
18. The *Electronic Visualization Laboratory* website, https://www.evl.uic.edu/info, accessed February 4, 2014.
19. Brown, Sheldon. "Introduction" in *Synthesis: Processing and Collaboration* (San Diego: The Gallery@Calit2, 2011) p. 5.
20. Wees, William. *Light Moving in Time* (Berkeley: University of California Press, 1992).
21. Lista, Marcella. "Empreintes sonores et metaphores tactiles" in *Sons et Lumieres* (Paris: Centre Pompidou, 2004) pp. 63–76.
22. Private email discussing this essay prior to publication with Jamie Fenton, February 6, 2014.
23. Private email discussing this essay prior to publication with Jamie Fenton, February 7, 2014.
24. Minkowsky, John. "Design/Electronic Arts: The Buffalo Conference, March 10–13, 1977" in *The Emergence of Video Processing Tools, Volume 2*, eds. Kathy High, Sherry Miller Hocking and Mona Jimenez (Chicago: Intellect Books, 2014) pp. 407–408.
25. "Jamie Fenton," biography webpage on personal website: http://www.fentonia.com/bio, accessed February 4, 2014. Also, the quote is from provided in a private email, February 7, 2015: "I was the lead software engineer on the *Arcade* project. I had 2 engineers helping me. Part of my role was to make sure that the hardware guys created a good design. Jeff Frederiksen was the lead hardware guy—he was and is brilliant (and a little difficult to work with, since he could change a design on a moment's notice). Right now Jeff is working at Apple on the *iPhone*. All this means I can point-out where in the code things went wrong."

26. Moradi, Iman. *Gltch Aesthetics* (BA dissertation, School of Design Technology, Department of Architecture, The University of Huddersfield, January 27, 2004) pp. 28–33.
27. Moradi, Iman. "Introduction" in *Glitch: Designing Imperfection*, eds. Iman Moradi, Ant Scott, Joe Gilmore and Christopher Murphy (New York: Mark Batty, 2009) pp. 8–9.
28. Schwartz, Lillian F. with Laurens R. Schwartz. *The Computer Artists' Handbook* (New York: Norton, 1992).
29. Youngblood, Gene. "Art and Ontology: Electronic Visualization in Chicago" in *The Event Horizon*, eds. Lorne Falk and Barbara Fischer (Toronto: Coach House Press and The Walter Phillips Gallery, 1987) pp. 323–345.
30. Brown, Sheldon. "Introduction" in *Synthesis: Processing and Collaboration* (San Diego: The Gallery@Calit2, 2011) p. 5.
31. Ramey, Kathryn. *Experimental Filmmaking: Break the Machine* (Burlington: Focal Press, 2016) p. 365.
32. Adorno, Theodor. *Aesthetic Theory* (Minneapolis: University of Minnesota Press, 1998) pp. 246–248.
33. Betancourt, Michael. "Chance Operations/Limiting Frameworks: Sensitive Dependence on Initial Conditions" in *TOUT—FAIT: The Marcel Duchamp Studies Online Journal*, Vol. 2, No. 4 (2002).
34. Kotik, Peter. *Music by Marcel Duchamp*, CD liner notes and recording, Edition Block EB-202, Berlin, 1991, np.

2 The Heritage of Materialist Media

"Glitch art" is ambivalent. It confuses the relationship of signal::noise, while at the same time establishing the glitch as a definitional precondition: it is an attempt to recover technical failure as the basis for media practice, putting it within the general history of Formalist art. Conceptualizing the critical function that a glitch (stoppage) *may* have requires a consideration of the linkages between glitch and earlier theories of media. This critical role returns, either explicitly or implicitly, to Theodor Adorno's aesthetics where the interruptive capacities of art produce an inherent criticism of capitalism that necessarily denies ambivalence by ratifying the audience as passive. His argument is a recurrent element in discussions of collage, found footage films and materialist approaches to media art, a foundation that continues with digital videos and glitch as well as discussions of recombinant techniques such as remix. These critical claims following Adorno are the specific point of contestation in this analysis of how critical glitches have been organized around, through and by earlier theories of critical avant-garde film practice. In doing so, it becomes possible to challenge the Modernist conception of a passive audience, enabling a Contemporary reassessment of critical meaning for heuristic approaches such as glitch. This recognition clarifies the importance and indeterminacy of the stoppage in constructing glitch art.

2.1

Experimental film praxis implicitly organizes Contemporary critical meanings ascribed to glitches, a factor in their interpretation that must be delineated before it can be challenged: in the 1970s, the formal emphasis on the physicality of celluloid produced by rephotography in particular (film grain, dirt, scratches, etc.) as well as the technical apparatus of film projectors (flicker, the light projected in the theater) are all features of technical failure for commercial cinema, but are the *substance* employed by Formalist media art to engage with conceptual issues of cinematic language, technology and form. These same elements are the focus of Kathryn Ramey's continuity between the formal heuristics of "experimental filmmaking" and glitch procedures. Filmmaker/historian Malcolm LeGrice explains the relationship between the elements Ramey explores and their formal/aesthetic significance:

> Fundamental to the concept of "Film as Film" is an equivalence to the modernist view that the meaning and aesthetic base of a work derives from its material rather than from an illusionist representation. Stressing the primacy of the work as material, as process, and constructing the aesthetic experience from the characteristics of the medium.[1]

The materialist approach unites different media through their attention to the encounter with the medium (the material) itself, rather than the fictional worlds created through media-as-dramatic-narrative. Earlier developments used to describe the avant-garde film and video art are thus instructive in considering the glitch. The development of materialist markers for physicality understands glitch via a Marxist critical role for art that articulates discontinuity as a challenge to capitalist protocols.[2] The distinctions between glitches deployed in film and those of digital media only differ in their technical generation/presentation—challenging the absolute critical distinctions between digital and analog images—Le Grice's observation that historically "the meaning and aesthetic base of a work derives from its material." A consideration of historical medium specificity is thus not only warranted, it can illuminate these problematics by identifying its origins in nineteenth and twentieth century critiques of capitalist production; acknowledging the continuity between digital glitches and materialist film undermines these Formalist aesthetics generally, inherently challenging the conceptual foundations of this critical framework.

Theodor Adorno's proposition of an inherent critical meaning/role for art theorizes any activity that draws attention to its material basis as critical. A focus on glitch as the material nature of technology is common to artist/writers on visual glitches, such as Iman Moradi in his thesis *Gltch Aesthetics* (2004), or artist Rosa Menkman in her book *The Glitch Moment(um)* (2011), converges with similar claims made for materialist media practices in the 1970s—the same time period when glitch video was being invented in Chicago—the self-critical refinement of cinema to the technology/material of photographic reproduction and film projection. Asserting the critical meaning for technical *imperfection* links Contemporary practices to earlier material markers in terms specific to digital technology. Earlier claims for materialist film by UK film maker Peter Gidal illuminates these Contemporary discussions:

> The concept of materialism cannot be covered by the concept and concrete reality of physicality. The attempt here is by fits and starts to elucidate a materialist process. The questions pertaining to representation-systems and codes has to do with the *physical* reproduction and transformation of *forms,* a reproduction, at some level, of the profilmic, that which the camera is aimed at—a transformation *to* the filmic, the filmic event, so to speak. This transformation has to do with codes of cinematic usage which for the most part are not clearly delineated in the case of experimental film. [. . .] This is in no way to say that which is materialist in film is what necessarily *shows,* or that it is camera, lenses, graininess, flicker *per se*, etc.[3]

Gidal's distinction between materialist and physical is necessary because what his theory proposes is a practice engaging with those features of photo-chemical motion pictures—celluloid film—converging on the same material markers that American historian P. Adams Sitney identified as the structural film. Both are concerned with a Formalist conception of cinema based in its technological particulars:

> The structural film insists on its shape, and what content it has is minimal and subsidiary to the outline. Four characteristics of the structural film are its fixed camera position (fixed frame from the viewer's perspective), the flicker effect, loop printing, and rephotography off the screen.[4]

The emphasis on *photography as a medium*, (as a specifically *material* process where the use of live action cameras to create an illusion of a recognizable everyday world on-screen), is essential to the materially based assertion of film *as* film. While these material elements are categorically different in origins than the digital glitch, at the same time they are commonly identified with technical failures—and have been used as material markers for revealing the physicality of their medium just as glitches have been used for digital media. The reiteration and repetition of this earlier Formalist approach in Contemporary work reflects the ongoing organization of productive and critical engagements by the recuperative aesthetics described by Terry Smith and C.B. Johnson. The heuristic uses of these materials as signifier for technical failure in commercial works follows a pervasive embrace of this materialist understanding of them as demonstrations of physicality.

Media historian and film maker Jackie Hatfield has noted that Greenberg's Formalist theory was not only the dominant conceptual framework after World War II, but that it is one that excluded any work violating its premises. The establishment of motion imagery—whether on film or video—as a field of serious academic and museal study codified already present tendencies, assorted distribution organizations and occasional exhibitions that had responded to Greenberg's theory. John G. Hanhardt, who was the curator and head of the film and video department at the Whitney Museum of American Art from 1974 to 1996, links Formalist art, Formalist film and realist film theory. Greenberg's Formalism, P. Adams Sitney's theorization of structural film, and Andre Bazin's ontological view of the photographic basis of film form a singular logical unit in his catalog essay for the 1976 American Federation of the Arts circulating film exhibition, *A History of the American Avant-Garde Cinema*:

> Structuralism attempts to locate the "universals," the "distinctive features," common to all of man's social and cultural expressions. In order to locate the distinctive features of film, the structuralist has modeled his approach on that of linguistics, which offers the model of linear, narrative forms.[5]

Hanhardt's approach indirectly references philosopher Stanley Cavell's book on cinema *The World Viewed*, a linkage made apparent in Hanhardt's title, "The Medium Viewed: The American Avant-Garde Film." This connection to Cavell's work brings the fusion of Bazin and Greenberg, both of whose aesthetics figure prominently in his book, explicitly (if obliquely) into focus. The construction of structural film—Formalist reduction—as revealing the inherent, *abstract principles* of cinema as *art* analogous to the formally reductive work of Abstract Expressionist painting give an historical end to the development of the American avant-garde film.

The photographic purity of structural film essentialized the role of the camera (and live action cinematography)—the influence of Bazin's realism—even if the finished, projected film in the theater constitutes an entirely distinct experience that brings re/photographic processes into the foreground. Hatfield identifies the essentialization of motion pictures as photographic representation (apparent in the structuralist film valorized by Sitney and in Bazin's ontology of photography) as determinant in how this Formalist reduction towards purity proceeds for media:

> In the second half of the twentieth century the history and theory of experimental film and video was written with a bias towards modernist material concerns stemming from Clement Greenberg's modernist

> position and material specific ideas. Similar to other art forms, a schematized formal history has been predominant . . .[6]

What Cascone noted as the "glitches, bugs, application errors, system crashes, clipping, aliasing, distortion, quantization noise and even the noise floor of computer sound cards"[7] all describe the digital medium in terms of its physical presentation, as *materiality*. This focus unites Contemporary analyses of glitch with the historically Modernist Formalism Le Grice describes as "film as film." It is revealed through Contemporary concerns with material markers for the physicality of the medium in question—the heritage of Greenberg's influence on avant-garde film in the 1960s and 70s continues to echo into the present: the conception of each medium as a distinct practice defined precisely by those effects that are unique to it becomes obvious in discussions of glitch-as-revelation of digital materiality. Cascone's engagement with digital sound where the affective *substance* of its re/production becomes equivalent to the *breakdowns* of that process is mirrored by the engagement with visual glitches as digital materiality.

Commercial production minimizes the physical elements of cinema; it directly rejects grain, dirt, scratches, etc.—all physical elements in film whose appearance is technical error for concerns with rendering the medium "transparent." These same elements' appearance in both the American structural film (Snow, Sharits, Frampton, et al.) and the UK materialist film (Gidal, LeGrice, et al.) reflects attempts to create a "counter-practice" for (critical) motion pictures, one organized by those aspects of the medium/technology normally minimized in commercial production: a heuristic where the glitches and technical failures become a counter-normative (critical) aesthetic. These material markers function symbolically as the materiality of production, demonstrations that the immaterial images of film (and video) are objects, rather than an illusory or transparent encounter with reality.

For the material substance—the base—of any image to become apparent, it must undergo a transformation from the material presentation of an image to the image itself—a transformation where the invisible base supporting the image change into the image itself. This change is the "making apparent" required for these material markers to emerge into visibility. It is a basic change of state, one that happens autonomously, but once it becomes *image* these material markers are subject to the same semiosis and order as any other elements in that image, a factor that Gidal notes in his "Theory and Definition of Structural/Materialist Film" in 1975.[8] This transformation renders glitch ambivalent because once it is visible *as* glitch, it is no longer only an autonomous process, it is also the result, the trace left by the process, linking the glitch to conceptions of photography as record.

The unity of ideation in this engagement with demonstrative record, whatever its source, reveals the convergence of these historically avant-garde techniques with their object of critique. Those practices that draw attention to technical apparatus, such as glitch, are a "technical failure" paralleling the approach P. Adams Sitney develops in his speech/essay "The Idea of Abstraction." Published in the magazine *Film Culture* in 1977, it is adapted from a series of lectures he gave at New York's Museum of Modern Art in 1971. The particular redefinition that his argument makes becomes progressively more apparent, as he quotes philosopher Whitehead in building his argument:

> There is a double sense of Abstraction in regard to the abstraction of *definite* eternal objects . . . There is an abstraction from actuality and abstraction from possibility." They run in opposite directions; from the physical situation there is a gradual purification of abstraction; from the idea of the possible (the realm of all possible things) the process of abstraction gets more and more concrete. [. . .] We all know, or have some general idea, what a narrative film is. What is its opposite? Narrative does not have a pure opposite. I postulate the word abstract, using it very carefully, as the opposite of narrative.[9]

Sitney's analysis of "abstraction" along the divisions Whitehead describes reconciles motion pictures that work to "divine the essential characteristics of physical things"—an ontological concern common to Bazin, Gidal and Formalist media generally—with what Sitney calls "the event," meaning images concerned with photographic reproduction as technical process, with motion pictures whose images contain live action photography.[10] This idea of film-as-presentation of "anterior action" unites these formal films with the same formal emphasis on the "generative" in digital systems. Glitch functions within this framework explicitly as *record,* but in place of the depicted, what appears is the process of that depiction.

Thus, while the *visibility* of digital glitches is the result of an unseen computational process being output for display on screen; the *actual* technical failure happens within that invisible process—it is always anterior to what appears on screen. This relationship between hidden process and apparent result organizes *Digital TV Dinner*: the glitch happens after the physical action, but before the visual appear. Fenton's explanation, "Popping out the cartridge while executing code in the console ROM created garbage references in the stack frames and invalid pointers, which caused the strange patterns to be drawn"[11] makes the generative nature implicit—yet the focus on visual glitches' criticality always depends not on this invisible process, but the demonstrable results for the audience encountering the work. It is the "strange patterns" that record the failure, presenting as glitch, that transform this unseen failure into visuality.

The digital glitch as a record indicating a particular type of failure converges with André Bazin's theory of photography in "Ontology of the Photographic Image." Predicated on film's photographic function as a *record* of events happening in front of a camera,[12] this understanding mirrors that of the glitch. Sitney's structural film transcribes Bazin's "ontology of photography" into formal concerns with reproductive photographic processes: materialist manipulations of photochemical and mechanical processes applied to *live action* footage that *re*produce those elements normally minimized—what are identified as technical failures or glitches in commercial cinema. Absent in Bazin's discussion is the mediating, generative role played by the sequential, toxic baths that chemically process exposed photographs into visual form. The necessity of a camera for the production of visual imagery is optional (if rare) in photography, a factor in the dismissal of the chemical-procedural foundations required for the generation of film images. Both digital and analog images have parallel productive systems, differing in material and method, but retaining the same organization of ACTION—PROCESS/GENERATION—DISPLAY as a bound unit necessary for the *existence* of any image.

Bazin's concern with photography as evidence of a direct link to its *ontological* source renders the conception of glitch-as-record demonstrative of the same field of potentials as in cinema, rendering the glitch realist in the same terms:

> Whatever the objections of our critical faculties, we are obliged to believe in the existence of the object represented: it is truly re-presented, made present in time and space. [. . .] Seen in this light, cinema appears to be the completion in time of photography's objectivity. A film is no longer limited to preserving the object sheathed in its moment, like the intact bodies of insects from a bygone era preserved in amber. [. . .] Only the impassive lens, in stripping the object of habits and preconceived notions, of all the spiritual detritus that my perception has wrapped it in, can offer it up unsullied to my attention and thus to my love. In the photograph, a natural image of a world we no longer able to see, nature finally does more than imitate art: it imitates the artist.[13]

The recognition of visual glitches (and glitch generally) as indicative of failure (but not the failure itself) is the ambivalent nature of glitch, it is both the evidence of a failure *having already happened* and the *form* that failure takes when it is encountered. Engaging the glitch-as-record of failure renders it a realist depiction of machine process, no different than more typical and common normative function; the glitch becomes transparent, evidence for the real failure within the digital system. Realism depends on this transparent presentation. Its role in commercial narrative rejects the intrusion of images' physical nature. The critical approaches developed by structural and material cinema become critical because they violate this role of realism in commercial narrative films; at the same time, their emphasis on film as fundamentally a photographic record then identifies its formal as a function of the material aspects of photography coupled with the projection of that film, returning them to the same issues of realism contained by photography-as-record.

These historical debates over realism, commercial cinema and materiality in film are relevant to digital media, especially glitch. This extension to address technical failures is logical because technical failures interrupt normative function; they illuminate the conditions for apparent critical function. Media art technologies in the 1970s, especially apparent in Tim Barker's historical discussion of their interrelationship with commercial production, prefigures these formal elements' transcription onto digital technology in the form of glitch. The error-as-record depends on acknowledging the machinic function of the system, even if conceptualized as malfunction; his article "Aesthetics of Error" shows these transformations in action:

> Rather than thinking of the digital event as the process by which preformed or pre-conceived *possible* information becomes *realized,* we can only think of an error as coming into being as unformed and unforeseen *potential* is *actualized.* The error is potential in the sense that it is not pre-formed or pre-programmed by the artists. It can only be described as potential, which is inherent in the machine.[14]

The glitch, to follow this logic, is a revelation of the *reality* of the machinic processes themselves, rather than an ambiguous result of stoppage that demands human consideration. Much as Bazin's "long take" enables the emergence of the reality of the events shown—this conception requires the digital glitch to be an autonomous emergence of the reality of the digital machine. Barker's theorization thus eliminates the role of audience (human) interpretation in the consideration of glitches in favor of ontology. Glitch as a "potential in the sense that it is not pre-formed or pre-programmed by the artists" renders it a *realist* presentation comparable to the material reality of cinema that is the concern of Sitney, Gidal and Bazin. The prominence of this theorization *as* definitional for the critical approach to cinematic practice becomes apparent in its pervasive use in theorizations where critical glitches become critical by drawing attention to the physicality of the medium via glitch (and technical failures generally), a claim common to Sitney, Gidal, Moradi, Menkman and Cascone.

2.2

The anti-decorative tendencies of both historical Modernism and capitalist industrial production reveal the link between "undecorated" art and ease of manufacture for unskilled labor, as well as the economies of production this rejection enabled through the embrace of Taylor's rationalized production techniques. The demands of capitalism for efficiency and speed of manufacture justify this elimination of decoration, complemented later in the century by a reduction to the distinctive features of the medium, linking these aesthetic developments to the productive demands of capitalism.[15] Duchamp's conception of the stoppage is critical of this scientific process by being both highly rational in its organization, and entirely irrational (idiosyncratic) in its significance. The rupture it presents is only incidentally related to the machine's deterministic function, drawing attention away from the autonomous process to the interpreting action that organizes it. The proposition of glitch within this context as a critical gesture in itself is necessarily compromised as it is complicit with its object of critique: the materialist reduction that renders the glitch critical is the same process that renders capitalist value.

Theodor Adorno's posthumously published book *Aesthetic Theory* (1970) argues that art is an inherently critical mode of production, where the emergence of the material basis of art brings the audience an awareness of the reality of its production. Because art violates the functional demands of bourgeois society, it is *inherently* critical; this argument is unacknowledged in glitch theory, but it reveals the "inherently critical" claim that organizes Gidal's argument. A critical conception depends on this revelation of artifice since critical meaning is an inherent part of his definition of art:

> Art, however, is social not only because of its mode of production, in which the dialectic of the forces and relations of production is concentrated, nor simply because of the social derivation of its thematic material. Much more importantly, art becomes social by its opposition to society, and it occupies this position only as autonomous art. By crystalizing in itself as something unique to itself, rather than complying with existing social norms and qualifying as "socially useful," it criticizes society by merely existing, . . . a denunciation of useful labor, the strongest defense of art against its bourgeois functionalization . . . the ends-means-rationality of utility. This is enciphered in art and is the source of art's social explosiveness.[16]

Adorno's argument for certain forms of media being inherently critical depends on a specific conception of art that places this concept outside of the social frameworks ("its opposition to society") that enable its identification: this dimension is readily apparent in his statement that art "criticizes society by merely existing" because, for his argument, art necessarily has no function. Art exists in a separate domain from use value: the bourgeois demand for *functionality* described by Adolph Loos's denigration of decoration as immoral links the signifiers of skilled workmanship to "wasted capital," thus lost value:

> The advancement of culture is synonymous with the removal of ornament from objects of daily use. [. . .] It represents a crime against the national economy, and as a result of it, human labor, money, and material are ruined. Time cannot compensate for this kind of damage. [. . .] Ornament is wasted manpower and therefore wasted health. It has always been like this. But today it means wasted material, and both mean wasted capital.[17]

Writing in 1909, Loos's claim of cultural development links his underlying capitalist objections to the role of human labor in the production of ornamentation: decoration requires skill and was associated with careful craftsmanship (i.e. highly specialized, trained labor) requiring more time than the production of simple, unornamented objects. The critical potentials for glitch (and art) as disruptive gesture in Adorno's argument lie not with the interruption of seamless progression, but as a demonstrative excess of production as glitch becomes a baroque eruption, beyond simply interrupting the productive flow, it can assume the character of this decorative wasted production, a position that moves the glitch beyond the scope of allowed functions within capitalism.

The historical costs for decoration were necessarily higher both in the quantitative terms of production time, and qualitatively through the requirement of greater skill (thus greater cost) for labor, as he notes: "The lack of ornament results in reduced working hours and an increased wage."[18] Loos's shift from capitalism to aesthetics[19] integrates the lack of skill required not only by Taylorism, (but inherent in industrial capitalism as Marx's description of uniform labor power[20] that identified value generated by the amount of time the least-skilled laborer needs), with a reductive aesthetic that comes to dominance by the mid-twentieth century. The elimination of greater wages means a higher rate of profit. The appearance of glitch as an indication of transformative *excess to* production (waste) brings the underlying concern with productivity into focus. Capitalist production's inherent focus on profit, rather than on this historically reductive process *per se,* returns as a counter-tendency: the recovery of lost production as new value. Adorno's description of the audience-as-passive depends on this conception of them as mere purchasers who are neither expected to question what they consume, nor allowed to desire anything that challenges their beliefs: the fluid interchange between positions of un/critical meaning acknowledges the expansive nature of capitalist claims on value.

The digital is dualistic—both historical and immanent: a precarious balance between *being* (result) and *being-made* (generated), that reflects the immanent, on-demand nature of its immaterial form/production, invoking theorist Peter Burger's observation about the problem of realism:

> George Lukàcs sees the task of the realist (as opposed to the avant-gardiste) as two-fold: "first, the uncovering and artistic shaping of these connections (i.e. the connections within social reality) and secondly and inseparably from the former, the artistic covering of connections that have been worked out abstractly—the sublation of the abstraction." What Lukàcs calls 'covering' here is nothing other than the creation of the appearance *(Schein)* of nature. The organic work of art seeks to make unrecognizable the fact that it has been made. The opposite holds true for the avant-gardiste work: it proclaims itself an artificial construct, an artifact.[21]

This failure is apparent as the on demand nature of digital production: the creation via the immanent generation of digital works is at the same time a paradox where their actual material substance as instrumental instructions for the computer's operations dissolves this foundation into the illusion that what is encountered as product is the same as the source of that production. This issue lies with aesthetic semblance (*Schein)*:

> [Herbert] Marcuse outlines the global determination of art's function in bourgeois society, which is a contradictory one: on the one hand, it shows "forgotten truths" (thus it protests against a reality in which these truths have no validity); on the other, such truths are detached from reality through the medium of aesthetic semblance *(Schein)*—art thus stabilizes the very social conditions against which it protests.[22]

This autonomous aesthetic, separate from social function, is internalized in digital capitalism as the "aura of the digital." Glitch emerges in this context as both constrained by its dependence on the technologies productive of it, and elided by those technologies embeddedness in the superstructures of digital capitalism they were instrumental in creating. The stripping of physicality from consciousness that is essential to this fantasy of capitalist expansion without consumption appears historically as the "white cube" of the art gallery where external distractions are eliminated from view. This elision becomes an internalized model for engaging digital art, a shift that assimilated earlier art theories to capitalist concerns. Berger's discussion of the problems with this critical aesthetic anticipates the embrace of the aura of the digital:

> [Herbert] Marcuse outlines the global determination of art's function in bourgeois society, which is a contradictory one: on the one hand, it shows "forgotten truths" (thus it protests against a reality in which these truths have no validity); on the other, such truths are detached from reality through the medium of aesthetic semblance *(Schein)*—art thus stabilizes the very social conditions against which it protests.[23]

The glitch has been assigned this role as Berger's "forgotten truth." The claims that glitches reveal the inherent protocols of the digital machine correspond to precisely this claim—the paradox for glitch is its apparent revelation of a digital truth is the illusion. When the material aspects of the media itself become "visible," they commonly fall into a binary duality, as either a transient failure that is promptly disassociated from the hypothetical ideal pure media—ignored following the aura of the digital—or it becomes a passive signifier of materiality. As with the physical aspects of the film material that are Gidal's *materialist film*—frame lines, tape splices, dirt, fingerprints etc.—the glitch can function as signifier for noise since, as technical failure it is noise that decomposes the apparent "perfection" of the commercial work. The transformation of this noise into a signifier for materiality reiterates the glitch under new terms, those of illusion (*Schein*). What this transformation of critique reveals is how the conception of glitch as technical error traps the glitch process in a position that cannot directly engage in a political meaning: the glitch in itself (without semiotic function) ironically cannot be a critical rupture. It elides the productive, physical nature of digital processes. This process reflects the aura of the digital's rendering the physical appearance of the digital moot: if the digital must surrender its relationship to reality, then there can be no critically engaged digital art; however, this separation is itself the illusion since the digital is not hermetically separated from the physical world. The aura of the digital appears to neutralize any impact of the social space and human conception in advance of its presentation in an unseen embrace drawing everything together into the network.[24] The style that digital technology promotes is synthesis[25] a consequence of its reliance on sampling and reproduction. It renders the glitch as a signifier *of* and *for* technical failure, rather than as stoppage or immanent breach in the system.

However, understanding glitches in these terms requires a passive audience rendered active by the disruptive effect of art. This simple binary relationship of active:passive is denied by the ways that the aura of the digital strips technical failures from consciousness, naturalizing them as digital artifacts that can be ignored. These "invisibles" for consideration are glitches of all varieties: compression, signal failure, momentary drop-outs. Critical interpretations based in this understanding of digital media are captured by *how* digital capitalism and the ideology of the digital develop from earlier theories of critical aesthetics. Disentangling these interpretations becomes an essential theoretical activity for any media praxis that seeks a heuristic capable of either critiquing Contemporary digital capitalism, or engaging its appearance in digital media.

The use of material markers such as glitches common to Marxist aesthetic theory depend on the *a priori* conception of them as inherently critical. In Gidal's proposal the critical meaning of glitches depends on their opposition to conventions of realism in commercial media; contradicting Gidal's claims for a "revolutionary" media based on a materialist Formalism, the history of this Formalism masks the demands of capitalism for reduced costs of both labor and production. It is this connection between the avant-garde and the industrial reform movements of the nineteenth century[26] that undermine any claims for a critical Formalism: the historical, reductive art/design illustrated by the claim of "form is function" employs essentializing interpretations dependent upon where the pure features of a medium demonstrate how the historical avant-garde internalized the deskilling of labor that accompanied this productive elision of decoration as an assault on traditional art; as has been the case since the nineteenth century, the arts are subject to technologically disruptive innovation first, with the avant-garde itself being an internalization of this process.[27]

The organization of glitches—even more than Gidal's materialist views—develops out of this heritage as their visible structures commonly reference the geometric character of historical abstract art even when their appearances employ/contain elements of realist photographic material. However, this transformation and linkage of Formalism and semiosis is a surprise since the historical configuration of these two approaches was in opposition, as historian Thomas McEvilley noted in his book *Art and Discontent*:

> Greenberg, for example, often uses the term "non-representational" to describe "pure" artworks—those purified of the world. But as he uses it, the term seems to rule out only clear representations of physical objects such as chairs, bowls of fruit, or naked figures lying on couches. [. . .] But art that is non-representational in this sense may still be representational in others. [. . .] This historical quibble is important

> because it points to a significant set of omissions in the Greenbergian argument—and the reasons for the omissions is not far to seek: in these older traditions content was read comfortably from abstract form. [. . .] They present two-dimensional models or schematic diagrams of the real; to call them diagrams of consciousness as then experienced, without altering the facts, would bring them into a more phenomenological framework.[28]

The abstraction of the 1950s and 1960s only superficially avoids the content of mimetic art—the recognizable appearances of surface realism—rather than the issues of content as they are produced through interpretation. Semiotic function does not necessarily result in a subsumption within an established system of meanings—it opens up the potential for roles that violate and disrupt these codes as the glitch is a dependent form, one that emerges in contrast to some other established ground.[29] Its ambivalence demonstrates and depends on a relationship that can either reinforce that established paradigm or violate it: this ambiguity destabilizes the established order[30]; its denial therefore acts to assert control over these aberrant potentials in advance of their appearance. McEvilley identifies the challenge that semiotic ordering poses to the fixed relationships contained by the evacuation of content in this art as a feature of the organization of these paintings—as a function of their semiotic relationship to other, earlier works:

> Ad Reinhardt also belonged to what Rosenberg called the metaphysical branch of abstract expressionism. [. . .] Critics seeking the content of his work should look neither to the Greek Christian cross nor to the problem of the surface, but to the four-limbed mandalas of the Orient—especially the Taoist mandala of 64 squares which is virtually identical to the internal quadrature of Reinhardt's paintings.[31]

The semiotic process opens the interpretation to metaphysical meanings; the linkages to this metaphysical content are apparent in the formal organization of the work—in their quotation, transformation and reiteration of the existing form of the Taoist mandala. This construction is an observable feature of the work: accounting for it requires a consideration of its parallels with earlier art, a linkage that transforms the assumed non-representational character of the paintings into a specifically representational, but non-mimetic, depiction of a metaphysical reality, as McEvilley notes. This transformation reveals the semiotic character of these works, suggesting that the assumption of an antipathy between Formalist and semiotic procedures is an error.

This logical fallacy is precisely the point that McEvilley makes in his discussion—that there is no antipathy between these approaches, except in how the critical arguments of the 1950s and 1960s falsely presupposed such a divide. Its elimination follows the diminished tasks of a materialist presentation.[32] The elision of visible forms particularly apparent as the development from Abstract Expressionism to Minimalism into Conceptual Art—in each case, removing "inessential" elements determined by an *a priori* definition of "medium" (or "art")—demonstrate the tautological dimensions of this logical form and its recursive progression eliminates different, competing outside elements from consideration.[33] The complicity of this reductive process with the reductive and fragmentary protocols of both cybernetics and Taylorism reveals their unifying concern with emancipating each field as an isolated language game that controls and organizes itself independently.[34]

These work are *not non-representational*, but *non-mimetic*, a distinction that clarifies the ambiguous role of semiosis in the theoretical organization and meaning of glitch works. Correcting this historical misconception decenters the materialist elements in the argument for a critical media practice focused on their manipulation; it shifts the role of glitch from being an active confrontation to the semiotic organization of the work as a whole: critical meaning, while confronted by the stoppage specific to glitch, is not dependent on the stoppage so much as offers a potential for critical engagement at the moment of stoppage.

This process does not necessarily resist the glitch as physicality, it continues *through it*—as McEvilley's discussion of Reinhardt's metaphysical quotation of historical mandala forms reveals. It is not the materiality that is critical, but the organization of the whole. Critical Formalism is an engagement that attempts to collapse the distinctions between an interpretive identification of signifiers with the material substance of the medium being employed, to capture the rupture that glitch potentially has for these established codes: the procedure is vacant—it replaces the intellectual potentials of interpretation with the immanent encounter. This foundation has the same immanent rupture as the stoppage—the resulting semiosis begins as a perceptual engagement, yet cannot be resolved without recourse to intellectualization and reference to the norms of abstraction—without a reversion into the semiotic procedures that the perceptual seemed to deny. In *Digital TV Dinner* this limiting role is played by the historical conventions of visual music. Unlike mimetic art where interpretations can remain within the perceptual realm of surface appearances, abstraction as Umberto Eco noted in his essay "Interpreting Serials" *only* addresses an informed audience:

> there is no conceivable naive addressee of an abstract painting or sculpture. If there is one who—in front of it—asks, "But what does it mean?" this is not an addressee [. . .] he is excluded from any artistic experience whatever. Of abstract works there is only a critical "reading."[35]

For an uninformed audience, the meaning of the abstract is entirely missing—it is metaphorically a confrontation between two speakers of entirely different languages. As historical works eliminated recognizable forms and mimetic imagery, their comprehension became increasingly dependent on the capacities of the audience to recognize and interpret the work—an intellectual engagement. The various meaning of glitch: as stylistic device, as surface signifier of failure, as critical challenge to capitalist value, as indication that the work is broken and should be discarded—are immanent. Disentangling these interpretations of glitch and the material elements of media demonstrates how capitalist protocols take aesthetic shape as the ambivalence of glitches emerges from an internal contradiction between the protocols of capitalism and the elision of human interpretation from that consideration. It is the necessary link of interpretation with the presentation itself that is productive of a critical meaning, not the material markers of the productive process or their presentation, but the choice the audience makes[36] when confronted by the glitch.

Thus, with the aura of the digital internalized in the interpretations of digital works, the earlier neutralization posited by exhibition in gallery spaces has become a function of the (active) audience dynamically interpreting that renders the political meaning of glitch contextual and contingent. It is an understanding that discredits the proposal of an inherent critical role for glitch: for this conception, there is a singular meaning contained by the art, which autonomously manipulates the (passive) audience. The anthropological role of art as a social status marker thus becomes central to the critical meaning: art is *a marker of distinction*. It serves to separate different classes into subgroupings whose *status* and membership in those groups is reflected by the art they embrace: art's *function* (and thus its value in capitalist terms) depends on this social context.[37] Both art and glitch are thus ambivalent, as their meaning is variable, dependent on social role, always necessarily complicit with any critique it offers. This focus and submersion of critical roles within their object of challenge corresponds to theorist Jean-Francois Lyotard's concept of paralogism, as he explains in *The Postmodern Condition*:

> Paralogy must be distinguished from innovation: the latter is under the command of the system, or at the very least used by it to improve its efficiency; the former is a move (the importance of which is often not recognized until later) played in the pragmatics of knowledge. The fact that it is in reality frequently, but not necessarily, the case that one is transformed into the other presents no difficulties for this hypothesis.[38]

The ambivalence of glitches demonstrates Lyotard's concept of "paralogy": their reversibility between complicity and rupture with their critical function, revealing their problematic nature as how to deal with the ruptures they present when those ruptures are so readily elided? The heuristic approach to glitch as a demonstration/emergent technical failure brings the pragmatic functions of interpretation into the foreground, making their role in the aura of the digital an explicit part of the shifting role for glitch.

His paralogism has a specifically critical role, but this critical potential is a result of the relationship between paralogy and the language games that make it possible: it is tied to the rules that enable its critical action, in the same way that glitch is emergent; the stoppage producing the glitch indicates the temporary nature and context-dependence of these relationships: they are always subject to cancelation and alteration. The implementation of such control structures in digital technology create the illusion of their autonomy as an inviolable nature, factors that amplify the importance of glitches rather than diminishing them. Their challenges to structures of control may be contingent on the immanent engagement of the glitch with the specifics of its appearance in a video work, but at the same time this appearance is governed by the same expectations derived from past experience: through this relationship their critical function can be recovered as contingent and variable—and thus capable of violating the controls imposed and reified by the aura of the digital.

2.3

Technical failures happen invisibly; their appearance as visual glitch is an indication the breakdown is not total, a complete collapse of the digital system. These other glitches—the unseen ones that emerge from complete system breakdown—also can have impacts on the visual form, as in Joshua Gen Solondz's ten-minute video *Prisoner's Cinema* (2012), but unlike their more visible parallels, these ruptures produce a literal stoppage. Composed from individual black, white and graphic frames, *Prisoner's Cinema* employs a powerful, rhythmic flicker drawn from the historical materialist films of the 1960s and 1970s, but depends on an invisible glitch for its critical engagement with this tradition. This video is not simply a re-production of earlier structural film. Its flicker produces involuntary hallucinatory effects by rhythmic alternations of what begin as a series of alternating black and white frames (in themselves productive of phosphene imagery) that are gradually interspersed with alternating, linear mandala-patterns.

However, these images are not the glitch in *Prisoner's Cinema,* nor are they in themselves critical. Only the interruption of continuity (stoppage) is *potentially* critical. The glitch that produces the critical meaning is unseen in the finished video. It functions invisibly as the *limited duration* of the work: the ten-minute running time is the maximum length the computer used to make this flicker film could support before crashing, a demonstration of Solondz's commentary on his video: "I hand spliced this project until my computer crashed."[39] The critical meaning of this integral, unseen failure is determined *not* by its appearance within the work, but by how the technical failure effects a stoppage, breaking the trance this video induces and challenging its transcendent meaning/form directly by interrupting its progression.

The term "prisoner's cinema" commonly refers to a specific hallucinatory phenomenon experienced in the absence of light. Its role in this video connects it with earlier visual music works, while at the same time linking these synaesthetic works with the structural and materialist films. *Prisoner's Cinema* provides a nexus where these historical traditions converge on Contemporary digital technology through the integral function of glitch in the video. The paralogy is presents is specifically critical of historical avant-garde film, challenging the interpretation of its apparently materialist forms *as* critical: video does not innately flicker as film does.

Those visions seen in absolutely dark spaces—most famously in the darkness of dungeons, the source of the term "prisoner's cinema"—caused by the human nervous system itself. Neuropsychologist Oliver Sacks devoted a chapter in his book *Hallucinations* to the phenomenon of "prisoner's cinema" in which he defined the phenomena as a result of sensory deprivation:

> The brain needs not only perceptual input but perceptual *change*, and the absence may cause not only lapses of arousal and attention but perceptual aberrations as well. Whether darkness and solitude is sought out by holy men in caves or forced upon prisoners in lightless dungeons, the deprivation of normal visual input can stimulate the inner eye instead, producing dreams, vivid imaginings, or hallucinations. There is even a special term for the trains of brilliantly colored and varied hallucinations which come to console or torment those kept in isolation or darkness: "the prisoner's cinema."[40]

The foundations of this hallucinatory experience has parallels with the allegory of "the cave" proposed by Plato in *The Republic.* But it is not just an allegory of imprisonment, as it has obvious parallels in the movie theater: prisoners (by choice or force), immobile, stare captivated at a procession of hallucinatory shadows on the wall, confusing the phantasmal visages for real presences. In Plato's allegory, it is the world that is the prison, all the things that are seen that are the phantoms—escape only being possible by an effort to move away from the world of visible appearance in exchange for an enlightened mental vision:

> The world of our sight is like the habitation in prison, the fire-light there to the sunlight here, the ascent and the view of the upper world is the

> rising of the should into the world of mind; put it so and you will not be far from my own surmise.[41]

It is in the retreat from the world of everyday vision that this enlightenment arrives—thus the "darkness and solitude is sought out by holy men in caves" as a way of blinding one's self to the phantasmal illusions of the visible world. *The cave* presents the reversal of normal expectation, just as it's encapsulation within the movie theater—the shadows projected on the walls are more vivid than our normal experience, its hyperrealism shows imaginary sights that seem more real and concrete than our own everyday lives. To withhold these images, as flicker films all do, is to turn away from the cinematic world in much the same way that Plato's allegory turns away from visible reality. The audience is the prisoner in this cinema. The formal and semiotic connections between synaesthetic imagery and questions of realism brings the dependence on glitch as *limit* in *Prisoner's Cinema* into a critical paralogy with the materialist practices employed in this video.

The dominant imagery appearing in Solondz's video evokes not the technical failures of machinery, but the internal and integral failures of the human nervous system; the same synaesthetic imagery that is the reference point for Fenton's *Digital TV Dinner* returns to its origin point in the neural "noise" of vision called phosphenes. Common to both prisoner and mystic, they appear spontaneously when human eyes confront complete darkness, as biophysicist Dr. Gerald Oster notes in his article "Phosphenes," published in *Scientific American* in 1970:

> Phosphenes can arise spontaneously, and they can also be provoked in a number of ways. They appear spontaneously only when the usual visual stimuli are lacking and particularly when the viewer is subjected to prolonged visual deprivation. Phosphenes may account for the "illuminations," the visions or the experience of "seeing the light" reported by religious mystics meditating in the park; they are the "prisoner's cinema" experience by people in dark dungeons; they may well constitute the fact behind reports of phantoms and ghosts. Darkness is not a requirement; only the absence of external visual stimuli is needed.[42]

These graphic, repeating patterns can be seen by anyone, and have an extensive relationship to the imagery appearing in abstract films.[43] These forms are the vehicle that leads from a vision of the mundane, physical world that is nothing but shadows of reality to an enlightened, interior vision—they visualize the dualities that structure *Prisoner's Cinema*. This video is designed to produce this neural noise. The hallucinatory images invoked through flicker are also re-presented on screen graphically. However, these "grey" frames

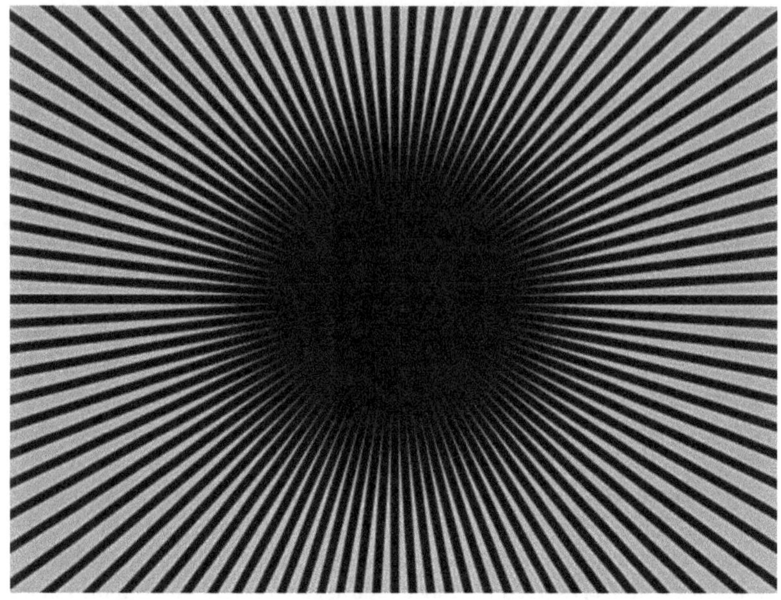

Figure 2.1 Still from *Prisoner's Cinema* (2012), by Joshua Gen Solondz

are *not* precisely grey—they are modulated, their implied imagery suggesting converging rings and rays, differences in density that converge at the center of the frame. When the radial images first begin appearing, [Figure 2.1] they seem to be emergent from both the white and black frames—a product of their interaction on the retina—as much as a physical presence on screen. It is only later in the movie, as they become more common, that their reality as image becomes certain. This ambiguity that transforms into an awareness of these radiant patterns *as* image is precisely the point: it is the shift from a hallucinatory perception to a tangible one this transition marks. The duplicity of hallucination/sight and transcendence/imprisonment are essential to the critical meaning of the stoppage. Historically the materialist cinema breaks the normal illusion of cinema—movement—replacing it with the audience's self-consciousness of their own immobility. (Duration becomes the material "on view.") The "movement" this historical cinema presents is a movement inwards, the metaphoric movement associated with enlightenment. *Prisoner's Cinema* takes this traditional understanding of the avant-garde flicker film as a given, challenging it through the evocation of this transcendence technologically—but this technical transcendence fails due to the unseen action of the glitch abruptly stopping its progression.

Oster's acknowledgement of the linkage between phosphene imagery and transcendence is a recurring aspect of how these perceptual hallucinations have been understood—this imagery has an extended history in avant-garde film as visual representations of this transcendence, a common refrain in discussions of phosphenes, not only in art, but in scientific discussions as well. The same forms that appear in phosphene visions also appear in other hallucinatory states, including chemical intoxication and synaesthesia. The metaphysical meanings attached to abstract art derive from the historical relationship between esoteric belief, notably the Theosophical Society, and early abstraction.[44] *Prisoner's Cinema* challenges phosphene's role as visualization of transcendence—as the imagery of metaphysical consciousness—by integrating it with a technical visualization which suddenly, and without warning, stops.

These relationships of esoteric metaphysics, Modernism and abstraction converged in the avant-garde experiments with "flicker films" in the 1960s, giving a second meaning parallel to the Marxist criticality of Gidal's materialist films that depends on dialectics. Philosopher Noel Carroll's discussion of these materialist tendencies follows the same trajectory as that of both Le Grice and Gidal:

> Created in the spirit of high modernism, these films were thought to reveal certain of the conditions of film viewing. "Flicks" or "Flickers," you'll recall, were once generic nicknames for films. So, these films were said to provide opportunities for viewers to come to understand something about the generic nature of film. And, in a less exalted vein, in the sixties, people also attempted to use flicker films to induce or accompany hallucinogenic experiences.[45]

Carroll's discussion delineates (and denigrates) two related avenues of development for the flicker film: (1) those works that reified their formal structure around the technical fact of intermittent film projection, in the process linking the pure experience of film to the material fact of celluloid and projectors; (2) the deployment of specific formal devices (such as flickering light) as an analogue to psychedelic experience linked to drugs and hallucinations, a variety of flicker he discounts as insignificant. When one remembers that "psychedelic" means "revelation of spirit," this linkage of hallucinatory states and technological apparatus potentially brings these flickering motion pictures into the same lineage as early abstraction in its action as facilitating a primordial, even metaphysical vision.

The radial patterns containing concentric circles appearing in Solondz's film [Figure 2.2] are similar to the naturally occurring phosphenes (particular to each audience member) that are triggered by the flicker itself. *Prisoner's*

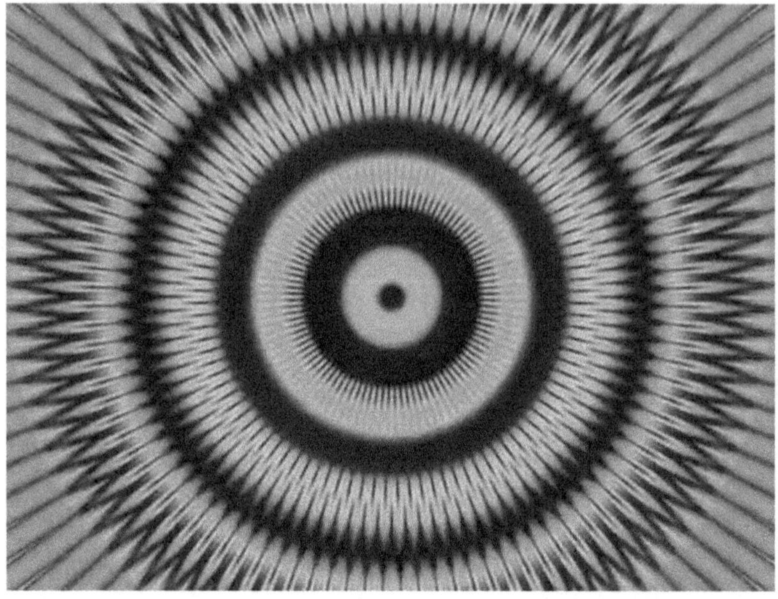

Figure 2.2 Still from *Prisoner's Cinema* (2012), by Joshua Gen Solondz

Cinema belongs to this second variety of flicker film, what LeGrice termed *perceptual cinema*:

> The term normally used for it is the 'flicker film,' though it is too specific to define it by a single characteristic rather than its region of function. This area is cinema attempts to examine, or to create experience through devices which work on the autonomic nervous system. Where the main characteristic of Op Art in painting is the use of simultaneous contrasts in sufficiently close planar relationship to stimulate an essentially retinal reaction, in film this reaches its purist form in a concentration on the temporal equivalent—rapid sequential contrasts.[46]

The neural noise of the human nervous system is an integral part of these images, a connection implicit in the origins of *Digital TV Dinner* and the explicit focus of *Prisoner's Cinema.* Both Le Grice and Carroll noted a link between Op Art and the flicker film. The repeating, radial imagery of these frames resembles paintings by Bridget Riley and Victor Vasarely, imagery composed from flat, graphic areas of serially repeating forms that appear in visual glitches. The optical effects of the combination of solid and pattern interact in strongly graphic ways on the retina, making the resulting imagery a composite of both after-image, hallucinatory phosphene and actual pattern.

It is precisely this engagement with a technological transcendence (induced) visualized through the neural noise of phosphenes that connects *Prisoner's Cinema* with the concerns of critical form in glitch work. The transformation of materialist cinema for digital technology brings these film as film procedures into dialogue with digital technology. This engagement with perception is not limited to the visuals; the droning soundtrack cycles through paired rhythms which, in conjunction with the flicker, induces both alpha and delta states in the human brain:

> Alpha rhythm refers to brain wave activity of cells firing at a rate of 8–12 cycles per second, a frequency associated with electroencephalographic (EEG) readings taken of test subjects during meditation. Researchers have found that certain cycles of flickering will induce these cells to sync up and fire in unison to the flicker frequency.[47]

Meditation practices are specifically focused on achieving the transcendent enlightenment evoked by psychedelics, abstraction and phosphene imagery. The radial patterns in Solondz's movie include the appearance of concentric circles that resemble mandala-forms. Their presence in this film is thus not surprising: the technical apparatus (cinema) that imprisons its audience is also a vehicle for their liberation, as Solondz explains about the soundtrack:

> It should induce alpha and delta states, the brain states of the hyper aware and the comatose.[48]

This conjoined pair—hyper aware and comatose—is a paradox, a superposition of two incompatible states that cannot exist simultaneously, thus inducing a struggle for dominance that is dramatized through the experience of watching *Prisoner's Cinema*. The integration of phenomenal experience into the formal organization of the work is a reflection of the heritage of earlier *perceptual cinema,* but at the same time is not a simple evocation and exploit of perception/experience—the struggle between mental states is at the same time a struggle between being conscious and unconscious. This internal conflict is the metaphoric struggle of the cave allegory: the "ascent into the light" that Plato describes is, in particular, a mental transition.

The experience of watching *Prisoner's Cinema* forms an essential part of its significance as the glitch that ends the video produces a convulsive stoppage for the viewer. The struggle between mental states is emblematic of the struggle for "consciousness of reality" associated with metaphysics: motion picture technology brings this conflict into consciousness without necessarily resolving the problem it poses. Instead, it is the *awareness* of struggle—that there might be a conflict between everyday experience and the metaphysical enlightened consciousness—through the technologically forced collision of incompatible mental states which is the central aspect of the encounter with this movie. The sudden shift to a white screen at the end of his movie, (a change where the pronounced flicker caused by alternations of white and black frames stops), can produce very strong phosphene images, but at the same time, it comes as a *break* in the clinical sense, a collapse of mental focus and the harmonizing of mental states evoked by the movie itself. The persistent phosphenes during this part of the movie are a reminder of the *failure* to transcend, which the static and pure white screen represent.

The motion picture technology employed in *Prisoner's Cinema* illustrates and brings the transcendent momentarily into consciousness as the meaning of the spectatorial experience without allowing the metaphysical experience to manifest. In its place is a representation (the movie itself) of what the process of transcendence is, but it is a transcendent that remains unrealized—the glitch acts to surreptitiously cut it off—in spite of its elaborate evocation and presentation through the technological apparatus, what transcendence there is in *Prisoner's Cinema* is confined to the duration of the cinematic itself. This limitation is the critical action of this unseen, integral glitch, forcing a recognition not only of the contingencies of transcendence, but the historically determinant form its presentation assumes in experimental films and videos. The critical meaning this glitch produces, while entirely dependent on the stoppage it effects is at the same time invisible *within* Solondz's video; no glitch appears, so while the work's critical significance comes from this glitch, the video is at the same time *not* recognizable as being a "glitch video."

2.4

The Modernist theoretical framework that argues the appearance of glitch forms in "glitch art" is an inherently critical activity originates with claims that technical failures of all types reveal the material foundations alluding to capitalist productive processes. A work such as *Prisoner's Cinema* neither supports nor challenges this claim, since the glitch in question is integral, invisible, structuring the work but not apparent in the piece itself except as an implicit and literal stoppage—the technical failure remains unencountered, is the *end* of the encounter. Instead, the critical claim made for these failures depends on their appearance in the work itself, thus enabling their recognition and identification *as glitch* by the audience. Gidal's theory of materialist film develops from the literalization of the "material basis of production" as those elements demonstrating cinema as a *material* form. Adorno's theory is implicit in the presentation of material markers as essential to critical activity:

> A film is materialist if it does not cover its apparatus of illusionism. Thus it is not a matter of anti-illusionism pure and simple, uncovered truth, but rather a constant procedural work against the attempts at producing an illusionist continuum's hegemony. Anti-illusionist materialist cinema is one which does not give the illusion of having dispensed with such questions. But such work, simultaneously, is not just a defensive practice against some hegemonic given against which it must constantly rail; it is not only in opposition, revolutionary.[49]

Gidal's heuristic focused on the productive dimensions of artistic action, not reception; the difficulty posed in discussing glitch aesthetics is they elide the audience from interpretation in favor of a false causal link between form and meaning, generation and reception, without concern for semiosis. This tacit embrace of *a priori* cultural givens in the form of "dominant" commercial cinema and a "resistant" critical practice produces his dialectic, but it also renders the critical as reflexively tied to that structure. A Contemporary work such as *Prisoner's Cinema* exhibits a paralogy that challenges these seemingly fixed relations.

Engagement by critical practice "in opposition" automatically and necessarily assumes, by virtue of its oppositional nature, a challenge simply by existing, a logical product dictated by its dialectical relationship to the designated "other," reiterating the form of Marxist critique. The materialist, formal elements of Gidal's conception are apparent in *Prisoner's Cinema.* It casts the audience as manipulated, passive observer[50]—a token (the literal/figurative "prisoner" of this cinema) that is controlled by the work being encountered. This conception of a passive audience is fundamental to Gidal's theory. His "revolutionary" practice is one where the alternatives to its form are rejected and ignored entirely as necessarily compromising the revolutionary position:

> The problem is that anyone can choose any "good object" and critique it, interpret it, by bringing out "what it is *really* doing." Thus analysis of *The Birds* or *Gertrud* or some Godard film or *Thriller* or *Jeanne Dielman* or *Daughter Rite* or *Born in Flames* resuscitates the object, reproduces its positions even if analysis is critical, demands it as a good object of desire even when, and in fact precisely when, contradictions are brought out. In that way, academic discourse solidifies the status quo of power and authority whilst ostensibly positioning itself (sometimes) against it.[51]

Any discussion of non-revolutionary works thus becomes inherently corrupting—compromised simply through the acknowledgement of their existence. This is a conception of audiences that renders their agency moot, passive. Audiences are given no ability to choose. There can be no challenge, no rejection—it is an argument that claims the only alternative is to render the opposed works *obscene*: beyond the scope of any engagement as they are inherently destructive,[52] a positioning that renders questioning the formal approach and its relationship to those forms equally impossible; it is a replacement of one hegemonic apparatus with another. Thus, media work is conceived as demiurgic, powerful, casting all its viewers as passive supporters—either critical or complicit, determined by what they are watching, not their engagement with it.

These dialectics are familiar. The characteristics that frame critical media as "truth" emerge from a presentation of the materialist basis of the work. While the particulars of Formalist media theories shift across theorists and over time, their common features become apparent in this constant return to Formalism. Film director and theorist Sergei Eisenstein's claims that the materials act as demonstrative of Marxist procedures through their formal character present the same dialectical argument as later materialist conceptions:

> According to Marx and Engels the dialectic system is only the conscious reproduction of the dialectic course (substance) of the external events of the world.
>
> Thus:
>
> The projection of the dialectic system of things
> into the brain
> *into the process of thinking*
> yields: dialectic methods of thinking;
> dialectic materialism—PHILOSOPHY
>
> *And also:*
>
> The projection of the same system of things
> *while creating concretely*
> *while giving form*
> yields: ART.[53]

Eisenstein's parallels between philosophical and practical deployments of the "dialectic system of things" renders their critique a function of formal organization that is necessarily critical of capitalism. This same externality—claimed for a shifting and varied collection of artists and works—is the formal basis that serves to guarantee its meaning by shifting the focus of interpretation from questions of semiotics to the discernment of the innate character and nature of the object itself, an empirical and final designation that appears to escape the problematics of interpretation simply through being *external* to them.

However, the designation of "critical" is not an objective description of the materials of the work; both Gidal and Eisenstein's dialectics contain the fallacy of false equivalence. The parallel Eisenstein stages and Gidal assumes is entirely an interpretation, a model that does not divine an internal order to the world, but rather one that imposes an interpretation, in this case the duality of not/critical, and then proceeds by defining a set of characteristics—what are immanently recognizable as a specific set of semiotic elements in the work—that produce such an interpretation. This argument does not escape this semiotic organization, instead becoming caught in the ambiguity of paralogy where the not/critical becomes reversible.

Revolutionary materialist art logically reflects the inherently critical claim created by the Marxist limiting structure. Theorizations of glitch (technical failure) as inherently critical adopt this conception of the audience's spectatorship as a *passive* activity. Contra Gidal, while media is always *interrupted* by the glitch because it is a technical failure, any critical meaning depends on the role it has when compared to other, similar works (the glitch's semiotic function within a particular work), not the *origins* of that glitch or its *a priori* role in an aesthetic designated *as* critical. Critical dimensions *only* appear at a moment of stoppage, as *Prisoner's Cinema* makes apparent. It depends on when an audience member *chooses* a critical engagement—i.e., *actively* engages it. Glitch art reflects paralogy through its ambiguous role in critical interpretations of media.

2.5

The problem posed by glitch's ambivalence, (dependent on its semiotic role in the work), demonstrates the contrast between abstraction and realism: mimetic art is apparently grounded by its resemblance to the everyday visible world in an immediate recognition of appearance; in contrast, the initial encounter with abstraction develops through the audience's past experience and knowledge of other abstract works. The dialectical opposition in Gidal is exactly this differentiation between realist mimesis and the materialist film.

Thus abstraction and representation are distinguished precisely because abstraction does not enable the instantaneous recognitions of an image's "contents." Depiction allows the audience to confuse this initial perception of subject matter with other types of interpretation, doubling its meaning as both representation and symbol: the immediate, direct "meaning," for example, in a painting by Paul Cezanne "containing" an image of an orange or a nude. Abstraction appears to lack such constraints since it is neither constrained by nor limited to the reproduction of readily recognizable forms. Understanding an abstract work depends instead on a fluency that is precisely culturally derived, and is not present at this initial level of perception/interpretation. Abstraction's dependence on *established* expertise—an abstract painting, such as a blue monochrome by Yves Klein, an artist whose works were concerned with the void, may not contain anything, yet is not devoid of meaning.

Duchamp's stoppage thus emerges as a critical example of paralogism, a questioning of this interpretive process. The interaction between glitch and normal function engages the controlling and structuring effects of established order. This dynamic relationship between recognition and interpretation organizes the glitches in Takeshi Murata's "datamoshing" *Monster Movie* (2005). The development of each shot/sequence depends on the recognition of the subject coupled with the glitch's capacity to shift from that representational image into abstract fields of moving color. The stoppage that emerges in this work is not a product of the glitch, but its instability between being-recognized mimesis and being-kinetic abstraction. Each progressive iteration of the digital glitch smears the imagery further and further from its source, until the end of each sequence, with its return to a momentarily recognizable image enables each stoppage to draw attention to the transformative action. Recognition becomes mis-recognition. In a glitch work such as *Monster Movie* established knowledge (past experience) is replaced by the immediate awareness of what was shown and its transformation into the unfamiliar. This process encapsulates the semiotic process of identification essential to interpretation: the audience's past expertise and familiarity with abstraction is therefore necessarily more prominent in the interpretation of abstract art.

The stoppage presented by the glitch reconfigures technical failures in both the new aesthetic and post-internet art as a transfer from digital technology into Contemporary art: the role of glitch and technical failures is symptomatic of the convergence between digital and traditional art,[54] in the process (simultaneously) normalizing these failures as a material demonstration of digital technology. The kabuki-like performance of them as symbolic criticism, a role bringing the glitch back into the realm of established function as *the* visualization of critical breakdown, a transfer that eliminates its action as stoppage.

Notes

1. Le Grice, Malcolm. *Experimental Cinema in the Digital Age* (London: BFI Publishing, 2006) p. 275.
2. Wees, William C. *Recycled Images* (New York: Anthology Film Archives, 1993) pp. 50–51.

3. Gidal, Peter. *Materialist Film* (London: Routledge, 1989) pp. 15–16.
4. Sitney, P. Adams. *Visionary Film: The American Avant-Garde 1943–1978 (Second Edition)* (New York: Oxford University Press, 1979) p. 370.
5. Hanhardt, John. "The Medium Viewed: The American Avant-Garde Film" in *A History of the American Avant-Garde Cinema* (New York: The American Federation of the Arts, 1976) p. 22.
6. Hatfield, Jackie. "Expanded Cinema and Narrative" in *Millennium Film Journal*, Nos. 39–40 "Hidden Currents" (Winter, 2003) pp. 63–64.
7. Cascone, Kim. "The Aesthetics of Failure: 'Post-Digital' Tendencies in Contemporary Computer Music" in *Computer Music Journal*, Vol. 24, No. 4 (Winter, 2000) p. 3.
8. Gidal, Peter. "Theory and Definition of Structural/Materialist Film" in *Flare Out: Aesthetics 1966–2016* (London: The Visible Press, 2016) pp. 40–52.
9. Sitney, P. Adams. "The Idea of Abstraction" in *Millennium Film Journal*, No. 63–64 (1977) p. 2.
10. Sitney, P. Adams. "The Idea of Abstraction" in *Millennium Film Journal*, No. 63–64 (1977) p. 24.
11. "Jamie Fenton," biography webpage on personal website: http://www.fentonia.com/bio, accessed February 4, 2014. Also, the quote is from provided in a private email, February 7, 2015: "I was the lead software engineer on the *Arcade* project. I had 2 engineers helping me. Part of my role was to make sure that the hardware guys created a good design. Jeff Frederiksen was the lead hardware guy—he was and is brilliant (and a little difficult to work with, since he could change a design on a moment's notice). Right now Jeff is working at Apple on the *iPhone.* All this means I can point-out where in the code things went wrong."
12. Bazin, André. "Ontology of the Photographic Image" trans. Hugh Gray, in *Film Quarterly*, Vol. 13, No. 4 (Summer, 1960) pp. 4–9.
13. Bazin, André. *What is Cinema?* trans. Timothy Barnard (Montreal: Caboose, 2009) pp. 8–9.
14. Barker, Tim. "Aesthetics of Error: Media Art, the Machine, the Unforeseen, and the Errant" in *Error: Glitch, Noise, and Jam in New Media Cultures*, ed. Mark Nunes (New York: Continuum, 2011) p. 52.
15. Lyotard, Jean-Francois. *The Postmodern Condition: A Report on Knowledge* (Minneapolis: University of Minnesota Press, 1993) pp. 60–62.
16. Adorno, Theodor. *Aesthetic Theory* (Minneapolis: University of Minnesota Press, 1998) pp. 225–227.
17. Loos, Adolph. "Ornament and Crime" in *Crime and Ornament: The Arts and Popular Culture in the Shadow of Adolph Loos*, eds. Bernie Miller and Melony Ward (New York: XYZ Books, 2002) pp. 30–33.
18. Loos, Adolf. "Ornament and Crime", p. 33.
19. Lears, T.J. Jackson. *No Place of Grace: Anti-Modernism and the Transformation of American Culture, 1880–1920* (New York: Pantheon, 1981).
20. Marx, Karl. *Capital, Volume 1* (New York: Penguin Classics, 1990) p. 129.
21. Burger, Peter. *Theory of the Avant-Garde* (Minneapolis: University of Minnesota Press, 1984) p. 11.
22. Burger, p. 72.
23. Burger, Peter. *Theory of the Avant-Garde* (Minneapolis: University of Minnesota Press, 1984) p. 11.
24. Reich, Robert B. *Supercapitalism: The Transformation of Business, Democracy, and Everyday Life* (New York: Vintage, 2008).

25. Poggioli, Renato. *The Theory of the Avant-Garde* (Cambridge: Harvard University Press, 1968) p. 125.
26. Kaplan, Wendy. "The Lamp of British Precedent" in *The Art That Is Life: The Arts and Crafts Movement in America, 1875–1920* (Boston: Museum of Fine Arts, 1987) pp. 52–60.
27. Betancourt, Michael. "Disruptive Technology: The Avant-Gardeness of Avant-Garde Art" in *CTheory*, 2002 (http://www.ctheory.net/articles.aspx?id=336).
28. McEvilley, Thomas. *Art and Discontent* (New York: Documentext, 1993) pp. 29–31.
29. Fer, Briony. *Abstract Art* (New Haven: Yale University Press, 1997) pp. 135–137.
30. Antin, David. "Have Mind, Will Travel" in *Robert Morris* (New York: Guggenheim Museum Publications, 1994) pp. 34–49.
31. McEvilley. *Art and Discontent*, pp. 34–35.
32. Fried, Michael. "Art and Objecthood" in *Minimal Art*, ed. Gregory Battcock (Berkeley: University of California Press, 1995) p. 125.
33. Foster, Hal. *The Return of the Real* (Cambridge: The MIT Press, 1996) p. 40.
34. Lyotard, Jean-Francois. *The Postmodern Condition: A Report on Knowledge* (Minneapolis: University of Minnesota Press, 1993) pp. 39–41.
35. Eco, Umberto. "Interpreting Serials" in *The Limits of Interpretations* (Bloomington: Indiana University Press, 1994) p. 98.
36. Eco. "Interpreting Serials", p. 92.
37. Willats, Steven. *Art and Social Function* (London: Ellipsis, 2000).
38. Lyotard, Jean-Francois. *The Postmodern Condition: A Report on Knowledge* (Minneapolis: University of Minnesota Press, 1993) p. 61.
39. Solondz, Joshua Gen. "VERSION 1PRISONERS CINEMA FINAL-no_credits-QuickTime H.264" https://vimeo.com/55609136, accessed April 23, 2015.
40. Sacks, Oliver. *Hallucinations* (New York: Vintage, 2012) p. 34.
41. Plato. "The Allegory of the Cave" in *The Republic*, Book VII, p. 3. http://hs.skschools.net/~malper/FOV2–00104A56/FOV2–0010546E/Plato%27s%20%22The%20Allegory%20of%20the%20Cave%22, accessed April 23, 2015.
42. Oster, Gerald. "Phosphenes" in *Scientific American*, Vol. 222, No. 2 (February, 1970) p. 83.
43. William C. Wees. *Light Moving in Time: Studies in the Visual Aesthetics of Avant-Garde Film* (Berkeley, CA: University of California Press, 1992).
44. Brougher, Kerry. *Visual Music: Art and Film Since 1900* (New York: Thames and Hudson, 2005).
45. Carroll, Noel. "The Essence of Cinema" in *Philosophical Studies*, Vol. 89, No. 2–3 (March, 1988) pp. 324–325.
46. LeGrice, Malcolm. *Abstract Film and beyond* (Cambridge: MIT Press, 1978) p. 105.
47. Salinker, Stephen. "Visual Responses in Perceptual Cinema" in *Journal of the University Film Association*, Vol. 32, No. 1–2 (Winter-Spring, 1980) p. 34.
48. Solondz, Joshua Gen. "VERSION 1PRISONERS CINEMA FINAL-no_credits-QuickTime H.264" https://vimeo.com/55609136, accessed April 23, 2015.
49. Gidal. "Theory and Definition of Structural/Materialist Film", p. 17.
50. Etcoff, Nancy. *Survival of the Prettiest: The Science of Beauty* (New York: Anchor Books, 1999) p. 217. Etcoff's comments are suggestive of both the relationship between the dominant group and their imitators: "The middle class are fashion followers, the most conservative of whom are dragged into wearing a style only because it has become so prevalent that it would be nonconformist *not* to.

The upper classes only fear being mistaken for their middle-class imitators, which is why they abandon a fashion as soon as it is adopted by them."

51. Gidal. "Theory and Definition of Structural/Materialist Film", p. 18.
52. Jancovich, Mark. "Naked Ambitions: Pornography, Taste and the Problem of the Middlebrow" in *Scope* June, 2001 http://www.nottingham.ac.uk/scope/documents/2001/june-2001/jancovich.pdf, accessed December 11, 2015, par. 48.
53. Sergei Eisenstein. *Film Form*, trans. Jay Leyda (New York: Harvest/HBJ, 1975) p. 45.
54. Paul, Christiane and Malcolm Levy. "Genealogie of the New Aesthetic" in *Postdigital Aesthetics: Art, Computation and Design*, eds. David M. Berry and Michael Dieter (New York: Palgrave Macmillan, 2015) pp. 27–43.

3 Digital *Mis*function and Materialist Approaches

Each time we encounter a digital artifact—either glitched or not, whatever its type—it is new, created specifically for the moment of encounter. Digital media is inherently a product of a generative technical system, the computer, producing the moment of encounter instantly. The mystification of the digital depends on precisely this immanence of creation. The immediate generation of works "on demand" has particular effects on how we engage with digital technology: it creates an illusion that the digital work is simply and only information, and what is rendered and produced in a tangible form at this point of encounter is thus insignificant, contingent, reflecting the fragmentary nature of the digital itself: everything "inside" the computer exists as binary data. The organized information replayed for a human audience appears continuous since its discrete units (commonly called "samples") are transmitted, reproduced and reassembled to become the encountered form of any digital media. This apparently prefect reproduction originates with the fact that the media encountered is not a *copy* so much as a new example made by the immaterial production of the digital technology specifically for the moment of encounter; the human-readable form is always immediate, new, an "original."

The "on demand" nature of this spontaneous generation gives what digital technology produces an "aura of information" that makes any particular work contingent, only a temporary print-out; the "real" form of the digital is never isolated in these physical encounters. Reassembly from fragmentary samples has enabled the rhetorical transformation of reality into data. The aura of information reflects the nature of digital technology as a semiotic system where each encounter has been rendered specifically for the moment of its engagement by an audience. This aura of information justifies the aura of the digital's stripping these physical encounters from our consideration—the failures of any particular encounter are simply transitory, not reflective of the "real" form of the digital object: information.

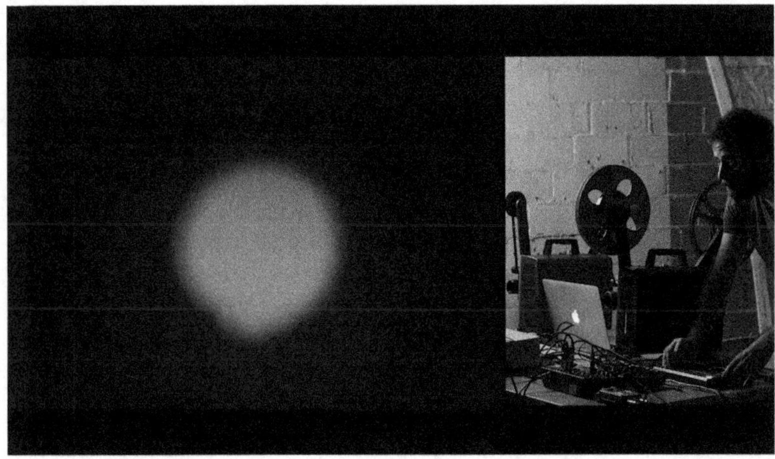

Figure 3.1 Screen and projectors from *Second Hermeneutic* (2013), by Michael Morris

A consideration of these dynamics illuminates the problematic aspects of the relationship between glitching and earlier analog "failures." The particular engagement with digital processes that informs filmmaker Michael Morris's expanded cinema performances makes the relationship between analog technology, the digital, autonomous datastream and human readable form into the subject of the work. The dynamic interplay between analogue and digital imaging technologies is the focus of *Second Hermeneutic* (2013) lasting approximately nine minutes, and *Third Hermeneutic* (2014) lasting approximately eleven minutes. Both pieces are live performances belonging to the visual music tradition that use a combination of traditional 16-mm film projectors and video; *Third Hermeneutic* also employs a laptop computer, a video projector connected to the laptop, a custom software created with the open source system Pure Data/GEM, a standard definition video camera, and uses midi to control the audio and video output [Figure 3.1]. Digital and analog imaging technologies exist in a continuum of approach that elides the technical differences between the different types of machinery. The "lack" of glitches in Morris's performances is thus irrelevant to their significance in illuminating the issue of digitality for critical media work.

3.1

Expanded cinema bridges the transition between historical materialist film practice and Contemporary concerns, not least with the "end of film." The same technical concerns with how digital technology relates to earlier traditions is apparent in the particular emphasis on technical failures of these mechanical systems as they now obsolesce and celluloid cinema becomes a historical medium rather than an ongoing and current, widely available and common commercial technology. In discussing this transition, Jonathan Walley's analysis of Contemporary revenants of the *film as film* ideology as the animating force of expanded cinema comes as a reflection how the new digital technologies problematize this history:

> The key to understanding these works is their preoccupation with the *difficulties* that the film medium presents: its clunky mechanical nature and resistance to ease of use. Also emphasised is the complex, component nature of film: the multiple chemical, mechanical and optical components and operations that require mastery, and the possibility of glitches inherent in each one.[1]

The spectral nature of this earlier technology remains apparent in the mediated and mediating nature of projection technologies that transform mere material into images. Rather than being a marginal phenomenon, the expanded cinema addresses the act and site of theatrical projection, bringing the elements of performance—and their potential interactivity—into consciousness.

Combining analog and digital technology is the focus of the *Second Hermeneutic* and *Third Hermeneutic* performances, even if it is not entirely apparent on screen: Morris-as-performer shares the space with the projected imagery, integrating his actions into what appears on screen. This presence of the projector/performer in the space with the screen aligns the presentation of his work with the performative elements in the materialist film work of Peter Gidal and Malcolm Le Grice. In *Second Hermeneutic,* the visuals are created by a pair of graphic animated films projected so that they partially overlap, the animated bands and fields of color linked audibly to the soundtrack in an immediately synchronous way—as something appears on screen, there is a directly audible response. This sound emerges from his use of the video camera's visual output run through his audio mix board to the speakers: it is an analogue sonification of the video signal. As a purely audio-visual experience, the performance might seem similar to such early expanded cinema[2] works as Paul Sharits's *Shutter Interface* (1975) where a series of four film projectors overlap their frames,[3] creating juxtapositions and combinations on screen—as in *Second Hermeneutic*; however, the difference is instantly apparent in the performance itself—the soundtrack emerges from the interaction of projected imagery resembling the bands and bars of an optical soundtrack, but with the addition of saturated color.

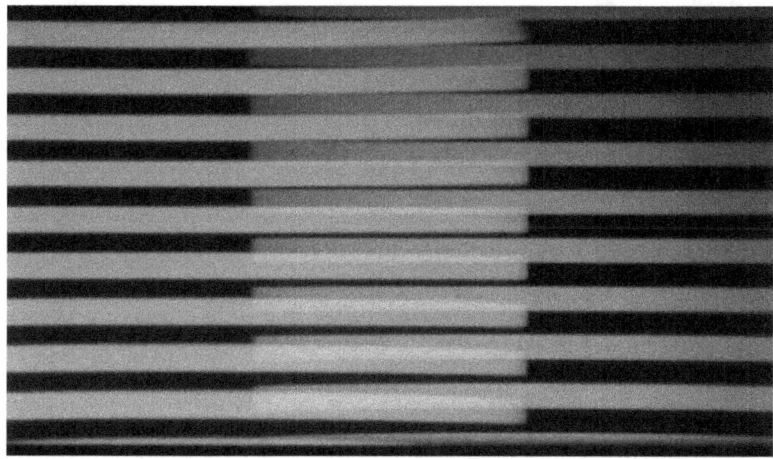

Figure 3.2 Interlaced film projections from *Second Hermeneutic* (2013), by Michael Morris

In this visual music performance, the animated bands' patterns provide the source for the soundtrack, reminiscent of historical films that visualize their soundtracks as their images, the same tradition that informs the recognition of *Digital TV Dinner*. This connection to experiments with creating images that mirror the contents of the optical soundtrack is no accident: the sound being performed is at the same time the images projected and interacting on screen: visuals become audible, mediated by technology [Figure 3.2]. The same engagement with historical approaches that Walley describes as a materialist engagement with celluloid organizes and renders Morris's works coherent as visual music. However, this same historical/technological mediation differentiates Morris's performance from earlier (yet similar) works: the soundhead in a film projector is simply a light-sensitive capacitor that translates light intensity into electrical voltage; when connected to a speaker, these electrical signals become the magnetic pulses which create vibrations—they become sound. It is an electrical system of transfer and translation that was developed in the 1920s[4] and, except for refinements of the technology, has remained fundamentally constant. This technology is *not* what Morris employs in his performance [Figure 3.3].

The word *hermeneutic* in both titles is a description of what's happening—the performance dramatizes a technological interpretative process—and an injunction to the audience. Hermeneutics are specifically concerned with interpretative processes, protocols and methodologies, which in the case of

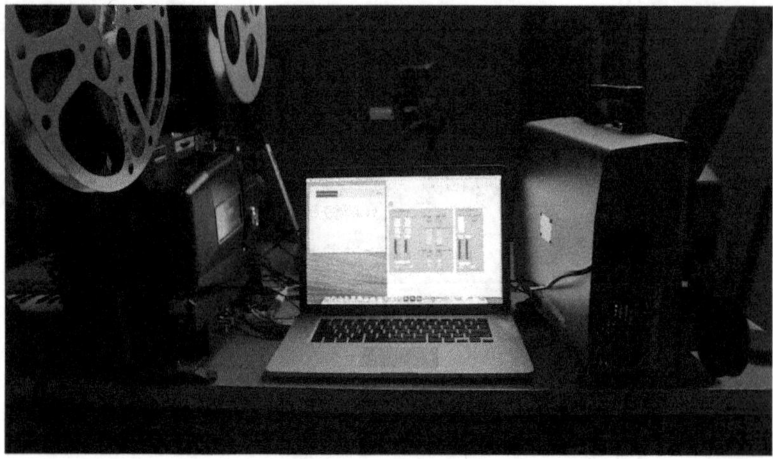

Figure 3.3 Custom audio patch in Pd used in *Third Hermeneutic* (2014), by Michael Morris

Second Hermeneutic appear in two mutually reinforcing ways, one technical and the other intellectual. The immediately obvious *hermeneutic* is the relationship between sight and sound: the images dynamically created by the two projectors overlap *is* the source for the soundtrack. The translation of the analog phenomenon into a semiotic material—the "information" of digital technology—the nature of digital technology renders video, audio or any other historical, established media as equivalents. The physical distinctions of media in digital technology emerge not from an innate nature, but from how the digital machine interprets their data sets following conventional protocols reified as the software rendering the file comprehensible to a human audience: "digital objects" become image, movie, text, sound, etc. *only* through software interpreting the binary signals that are the digital object. This decoding must follow an interpretative schema built-in to the software/machine to render this binary code into each human readable (superficially distinct) form; it is a semiotic process of immanent, automated facture.

This decoding process creates the aura of information around digital objects; however, semiosis is error-prone, and the prescriptive language of digital technology exhibits a sensitive dependence on the particulars of data—a factor that increases dramatically with compressed data—even minor errors can produce dramatic effects in the human readable form. This sensitivity becomes literally audible in *Third Hermeneutic.* The screaming, rhythmic noise of this performance is the transcription from not just one system (visual) to another (audio) but the interaction of digital imaging with analogue presentation.

So long as the instructions (digital object) remain legible to the digital system, it will function normally and generate a human readable form. Considering the *datastream* (information contained by/in the digital file) as the fundamental material for digital art—makes the emergence of *glitch art* as a formal demonstration of the datastream inevitable. The fundamental issue analysis of the glitch is the status or role of the audience interpreting the glitch itself. Digital failures in particular have become a common part of our collective experience of digital media, in part due to the rise of the internet in the 1990s as a mass medium, and partly due to their employment in art and music produced since that decade. Instead of being an exceptional occurrence, glitches are a commonplace part of using digital technology.

The interpreted nature of the digital sound/image is the focus of Morris's expanded cinema performances, dramatically connecting glitch to historical film practices: digital interpretation appears centrally in these works. Where traditional optical sound is a combination of electrical and mechanical technology, the system creating the sound in *Second Hermeneutic* is a hybrid system that employs a video camera to "see" what appears on screen, and then processes the video into sound. Because the transfer between image and audio is based in the variable voltages of the camera's output, it is similar to traditional analog process. *Third Hermeneutic* employs a digital translation to create its sound via software, the output could take on any form: unlike optical sound, an analog process. Morris created a custom processor using the open source programming environment *Pure Data* (Pd) to construct a sonification patch which turns the video image into audio wave forms that are then played:

> *Pd* is a so-called data flow programming language, where software called patches are developed graphically. Algorithmic functions are represented by objects, placed on a screen called canvas. Objects are connected together with cords, and data flows from one object to another through this cords. Each object performs a specific task, from very low level mathematic operations to complex audio or video functions such as reverberation, fft transform, or video decoding.[5]

The assembly of this software processor enables the shifting relationship between visual and audible, but the transfer is of an entirely different nature than the analog recording employed in historical optical sound. Where the densities producing sounds in an optical soundtrack are a physical remainder of an electrical response to light (much as the photo-chemical images of film are the response to light), in a digital system the data is a numerical sampling of these responses—a *symbolic* representation of an analog response, rather than the actual response. The computer depends on sampling for its presentation of analog phenomena (light reflected off a screen) as a series of discrete and uniform mathematical expressions of value: the imagery on screen could be of any type so long as its digital form created similar numerical values. The analogical relationship between pattern and sound in analogue technology becomes mediated in digital sampling, transforming it from physical relationship to a product of an autonomous interpretation. This difference between analog and digital means that the digital is always an *interpretation* while the analog is always more like a *footprint*—physically linked evidence of the original source, a direct record of physical action. Only the glitch challenges this separation by being a record of digital *mis*function, the product of partial and incomplete failure. The analog connection to a physical source is replaced by the *interpreted* nature of digital works—even the glitch-as-record remains an *interpreted* output of digital processing—this technical/aesthetic change is demonstrated by the pulsating, flowing imagery and soundtrack in *Third Hermeneutic*.

3.2

The aura of the digital's separation of the physical and digital dimensions of digital art from consideration is especially pronounced with media works; user-audiences for these technologies rarely become concerned by the interruptions posed by technical failures: just as the aura of the digital serves to strip the physical dimensions of media from consideration, the identification of these digital artifacts as glitches equally insures that they vanish from consciousness, naturalized as momentary (transient) failures in an otherwise functional system. This role for glitch as a catastrophe of digital technology is contingent on its identification as distinct from the regular function of that same system—the distinction between them relies on the normative discursive system of commercial media where the means of production disappears from the consideration of its products. Morris's performance work draws attention to these aspects of the digital, placing them in a direct continuum with earlier analogue film technologies. The glitch emerges as discontinuity, catastrophe, interruption—but only potentially present; glitch thus belongs within the same dynamic of recognition and elision that film historian Catherine Russell identifies for collage and assemblage—approaches employing self-evidently fragmentary assembly—employing the same process of rupture as glitch:

> If catastrophe is about sudden interruptions of a continuous system, it is at once produced by a system such as televisual flow and perpetuates it

> as a nonnarrative temporality. Unlike crisis, catastrophe is about instantaneousness and shares with "information" an urgency and forgettability.[6]

All these aberrant and unexpected results of catastrophe are examples of "glitch"; their forgettability is the totalizing impact of the aura of the digital in structuring and organizing the hierarchies of perception. What is noise and what is significant follows from initial and instantaneous choices about *what* is being encountered: the paralogical instability of glitch—belonging both to transitory interruptions and integral damage—has a dualistic result, challenging critical function by being complicit with the systems it critiques. These critical dynamics are reiterated across the range of critical forms—as a whole—collage, montage, appropriation, expanded cinema, glitch; Russell's theorization is typical of critical media. The arguments for critical media are remarkably consistent in their reliance on Adorno and his dialectics, marking the need to distinguish critical materialisms from their non-critical similars. Paralogical form is problematic, challenging stability and assumptive hierarchy by eliding its differences; its embrace marks the separation from Modernist aesthetics and simplistic dialectical form.

The term "glitch art" is another example of this need to distinguish between critical and non-critical. Theorists of glitch employ "glitch art" to distinguish between the specific *use* of glitches in an artwork, and those happening *spontaneously* in non-art contexts/works. Various writers on glitch art have proposed terms to identify this ontological distinction between a transitory technical failure (always called "glitch") and other variants designated differently, but which may have the same form: "glitch-alike" (Morandi), "domesticated glitch" (Menkman); what is identified with the term "glitch art" is a reflection of how artists have produced and exploited the "errors" emergent in digital technology. These qualifiers attached to the more generic term "glitch" are meant to signal the distinction between the transient technical failures appearing in typical media and those produced as artworks. It is a contextual distinction—separating works shown within an art context of some type, whether a gallery, festival or other location where glitched works would be readily recognized *not* as technical failures but as a feature of the work in question—that is at the same time used as a formal identifier, a way to separate those art works from *mere* technical failures. This distinction is itself problematic as it marks a difference that is not necessarily apparent in the glitch itself.

Mark Amerika's project *The Museum of Glitch Aesthetics* is both a website and print catalog. It documents the persona of "The Artist 2.0":

> the eponymous figure whose early 21st century oeuvre is featured online in the *Museum of Glitch Aesthetics* (MOGA). Presented as an "open

> persona" whose practice is a composite of hundreds of artists and hactivists all over the world, the story of The Artist 2.0 is playfully documented via the experimental transmedia narrative created by artist Mark Amerika as a new commission for the Abandon Normal Devices festival in the Northwest of England in conjunction with the London 2012 Olympics and Cultural Olympiad.[7]

The project presents a multiple, variant and discontinuous engagement with curatorial and museological form, most particularly exhibition and documentation in catalogue form. The list of visual works reproduced in the catalogue provide a range of imagery common to what James Bridle identified as "New Aesthetic": glitches of all types—encoding errors, pixilation, scan lines, digital noise.[8] It is an exhibition where the materiality of digital technology is clearly on display:

> The glitch aesthetic, at least in the context of what this entire museum project is founded upon, relates to the minor disturbances—intentionally executed or not—that disrupt the flow of data for aesthetic effect.[9]

The dismissal of differences between "glitch" and "glitch art" effected in *MOGA* are complicated by the particulars of context as a museum exhibition. The need to designate some glitch forms as *non-art* can be ignored rhetorically because the museal site has already rendered this distinction apparent *as* the exhibition/project itself. Any glitch that might find presentation in this context is automatically and necessarily rendered "art" because of its siting within the exhibition, within the art-making context of the museum—there is nothing novel about this dynamic; it has been an active part of the art world since at least the 1960s. Informing and elucidating problematics surrounding glitch, this project makes them its focus, drawing attention to the assimilative dimensions of aesthetic form when confronting digital technology. Glitch becomes in this context a signifier for the difficulty posed by anonymous and group-based production enabled by internet communication. What *MOGA* challenges is not those concepts focused around/by visual glitches, but the priorities of museumification and the organization of in/significant history.

In contrast to Mark Amerika's engagement with the aesthetic context in *Museum of Glitch Aesthetics*, Rosa Menkman follows a more Formalist approach in her *Vernacular of File Formats* (and its accompanying exhibitions). The concern with distinctions between mere technical failure, the use of it in art, and those forms that simulate such failures represents an attempt to establish glitch as distinct from commercial forms that simulate it: its use in the design of *IDN* magazine's "glitch issue" in 2011 recalls both the technical failures on display in their coverage as well as graphic designer David Carson's pioneering "grunge" designs of the 1990s.[10] Separating glitch from these forms is an attempt to define it in critical terms distinct from *style* or *fashion* in a denial of paralogy. Her project describes a morphology of glitches created by digital technology that develops from and asserts an imaginary formative distinction between "glitch" and "glitch art." Her project is precisely tautological in its description/identification of "glitch art": it dramatizes the tendency to identify and discuss only those glitches placed and exhibited in an art context, yet in its formulation and address implies a general applicability.[11] The *Vernacular of File Formats* is thus typical of how "glitch art" has been constructed as a critical practice, developing and elaborating a purely formal engagement with glitches. Her project demonstrates the dependence of this approach on definitions of necessary and sufficient characteristics for any given medium. The particular technical means of achieving each glitch is the subject of a careful study and examination, which is then formally documented as the essential element to the work/presentation. As with the other glitch presentations and explorations visible online, Menkman's *Vernacular of File Formats* is organized as a taxonomy that identifies and describes specific failures and their results when rendered by digital technology in a programmatic fashion.

The emergent dominance of semiosis and semiotic processes between the 1950s and the present is immediately obvious in the productive and analytic protocols of digital technology. However, this dominance is not limited to the immaterial production characteristic of the manipulation of databases by digital computers; it is reflected in the particular configuration of the Contemporary as an immanent, continuous—yet static—theoretical construction where there is neither a historical past or a potentially disruptive, unanticipated future. What theorist C. B. Johnson has identified as "modernity without a project" is a description of what appears to be a Modernist avant-garde lacking any concern with futurity:

> The era commencing in the 1990s, and intensifying in the 2000s, has consensually junked reference to the modern and the postmodern for "the contemporary". [. . .] "The contemporary" has a polemical power and induces undying sense of nowness. This was modernity: a time that oversaw vastly different ideological movements all trying to bring their own visions for the future into being, however opposed, ghastly, or desirable. It was the last time that society really believed in a future that was grasped as better than the present. [. . .] Modernity was relatively planned and directed, Post-Modernity continued in critical reference to the admittedly failed plan and direction of Modernity, but

> contemporaneity has abandoned the notion of modern life as one lived within a project centered around realizing any model of a future.[12]

The collapse of futurity that Johnson identifies, and the period in which it comes into dominance, mirrors the emergence and dominance of digital capitalism and the shift to semiotic production produced by this transition. His description of the Contemporary coincides with the aftermath of the twentieth century: the ruins of both Modernism and Post-Modernism dominate an intellectual landscape defined by recovery, reconstruction and the rehabilitation of the historical past—what is identified with the Contemporary. It is a space of wreckage and dissolution where the clearing-away inaugurated by the avant-gardes have not so much cleared space as rendered the past derelict: an assortment of unrelated, fragmentary ideologies and aesthetics whose organization appears as pointless as it is necessary.

Art historian Thomas Crow's observations about Contemporary art published in 2000, fifteen years before Johnson, anticipates his critique in *Modernity without a Project*. The conditions Crow describes align with digital technology's transformation of history into immanence:

> Almost every work of serious contemporary art recapitulates, on some explicit or implicit level, the historical sequence of objects to which it belongs. Consciousness of precedent has become very nearly the condition and definition of major artistic ambition.[13]

Contemporary rejection of futurity (essential to the historical avant-garde[14] tradition) is a major shift. The historical background to Contemporary work—those aspects of the art of the past which artists draw upon and reuse in the creation of their work—renders all Contemporary work within the range of recombinant practices, what Eduardo Navas calls "remix" and which is well known as collage, montage or assemblage generally. This self-consciousness is a *historical* consciousness. It reflects the conception of culture as database in a transfer between digital technology and the model-conception of cultural action/production. This process acknowledges that once digitized, all cultural production—art, literature, history—become data points which liquidates their differences (temporal, spatial, cultural) in favor of a generalized relativity where the meaning of the work is rendered (literally) insignificant.[15] It justifies the appropriation of symbols, forms and devices from any period within a single work—a multi-cultural colonialism,[16] performed without consideration of the contradictions and conflicts of such assemblages, hallmarks of an ahistorical conception of these materials common to digital capitalism's immanent presentations reflecting the random access nature of the database. Johnson elaborates on this elision of differences, linking them explicitly to the developments of digital, networked society—to the emergence of digital capitalism:

> In high modernity, life was still organised into two distinct temporalities: the city and the countryside. In the contemporary, major technologies such as cyberspace—which William Gibson famously defined as a "consensual hallucination experienced daily by billions of legitimate operators, in every nation. . . . A graphic representation of data abstracted from the banks of every computer in the human system. Unthinkable complexity"—help to obliterate temporal lagging, and remake the most rural lands in the image of the urban.[17]

Reassembly from fragments invokes this semiosis, but it also implies the transformation of unified, complete objects into fragments. The model this development implies is *collage* rather than invention or creation; quotational and semiotic in praxis. This compartmentalization and break-up into pieces (samples, pixels, etc.) suggests a quotational organization of materials. However, the issue of quotation common to recombinant media and assumed in the Formalist approach employed by Menkman et al. is problematic as it depends on the audience *recognizing* the repeated elements and reflecting on their use of past experience in making that identification. The Contemporary recuperates these processes via the linguistic play of quotation, schema and reiteration common to semiosis, a recovery that is simultaneously grounded in history and an ahistorical collapse into *presentness* that aligns with the immanent "on demand" production common to digital technology. It results in an all-encompassing equivalence denying differences; it is fundamentally the condition of semiotic production specific to digital capitalism.

3.3

The immanent production of digital media—every encounter with a digital work is always *new*, in relation to something generated immediately (on demand) for the current encounter—apparent content of this hypothetical glitch becomes irrelevant. It could be a photograph, typography, or simply a collection of linear elements—because any type of image can be stored in one of these three ways. Consider this hypothetical situation involving three apparently identical images for their human audiences:

(a) an uncompressed raster file specifying each and every pixel displayed;
(b) a compressed version of the same raster data;
(c) a version of the same image, but produced and described using vector graphics in which no pixels are specified.

The human-readable products of each of these three images are identical, so completely similar that there is no difference between the human-readable form for any of these images: they appear more than similar, to their human audiences (a), (b) and (c) are so completely identical that they are the same; it is impossible for a human observer to distinguish between them based on their human-readable form. However, despite being apparently identical, each of these is an individual, separate and unique digital object resulting from entirely different procedures and instructions. This technical difference remains the case with these images no matter how frequently they are rendered as human-readable images, or the individual files are copied or otherwise reproduced as digital files.

This hypothetical example makes the foundation of digital facture and its connections to the aura of information apparent since to human audiences, the tendency is to believe that these human-readable images are products of the *same data*, not just similar results originating with distinct and unique datasets. This idea that all three of these images are *actually* the same is an illusion created by the aura of information. It is this aura—that all digital information remains constant, equivalent no matter what types of transformations are applied (in this case both compression and the distinctions between raster and vector storage of image data)—that mystifies digital production. Each rendition of digital code as an identical human readable object (the apparently identical image) encourages a belief in the equivalency between distinct data files each containing unique, divergent code, that reflects the aura of information in action. The equally mistaken belief that re-rendering (not re-compressing) compressed files results in their gradual degradation follows from this same error.

As the aura of information demands, categories of glitch can be, and in artistic practice often are indistinguishable: semiotic processing renders the entire distinction between glitch and glitch art questionable, as artist Curt Cloninger observed in *The Glitch Reader(ror)*—the separation of the two as phenomena is complicated by the ambivalence of these terms themselves:

> The term 'glitch art' might apply to all domesticated glitches and all wild glitches that have been 'captured' and recontextualized as art.[18]

The "might" opens the potential scope of glitch art beyond simply those glitches captured in a recording to include actual technical failures, "wild glitches," orchestrated to occur on demand within a specific performance; thus, the distinction between an unpremeditated technical failure, unstable and transitory, and the use of audio-or-visual artifacts that coincide with these incidental errors, stable and repeatably a part of a finished work may be difficult to identify when encountered. The origins of any particular glitch are not necessarily apparent in it because the meaning presented by a work is separate from the physical representation of that work. The accompanying and implicit denial of the distinctions between human and machine readable objects, as with the passive conception of audience, all emerge from the same Modernist foundation.

These fragmented, recombinant media all depend on the development of digital technology that enables a precise control over the individual sampled elements. While earlier technologies of image transmission employed similar means to the digital fragmentation—technical processes that become digitized as computer technology develops—earlier systems such as Ernest Hummel's "telediagraph," a technology to transmit photography over distances for newspaper reproduction in the 1890s and its refinements in later decades as "wired photography," do not enable the precise control over images that their development eventually enables. This device uses a fragmentation procedure common to digital technology: the image to be transferred is divided into discrete elements (halftone dots are analogs for pixels) which are then sent in continuous sequence accompanied by information about when a line of dots ends, thus enabling their reassembly into a coherent image.

The distinction between this early invention and Contemporary digital technology is vast, yet they operate from the same underlying principle of fragmentation and subsequent reassembly. Each new reproductive technology reinvents this process under a new name; one of the features of "new media" is this consistent paradigm based in semiotic reuse and reassembly—a reorganization of already existing production, whether the approach is named collage, montage, remix, appropriation or anything else—its visibility in the art is dependent on the availability of reproduced work, the ease of technological access and application, and the availability of supportive exhibition spaces to show the results. Digital technology enables the precise control over each particular sample in itself, redefining this history of analog technology as an *anticipation* of what became possible with the digital computer.

The procedure employed in Hummel's machine necessarily produces a simplification of the imagery it transmits: any information not contained by the samples—information that exists in between the individual fragments, elided by the fragmentation process itself—does not exist in the resulting data record; this issue of information lost in the sampling process is compounded by compression algorithms in digital technology. Yet their organization in a finished work follows an *a priori* protocol governed by specifically semantic forms—both the analog and digital variants of sampling are a semiotic system. The distinctions between them are less an issue of technology than one determined by the capacity to manipulate the samples individually.

The immobility of analog samples reflects their material (physical) nature as analogues to other, physical phenomena: the trajectory of sampling technologies in the twentieth century culminates in the digital computer's capacity to manipulate and adjust the interior elements of the samples themselves. This transition enables the immaterialist conception of digital technology as transcending the physical constraints. The 'unmasking' that glitch appears to perform—via stoppage—develops from a confusion of operation of the digital machine with the codes that organize its automated facture. The aura of the digital enables the contradictory claim of the immaterial becoming manifest—of the state of information being realized in a direct, tangible form—via the instrumentality of digital technology. This reification transforms digital technology into the embodiment of an immaterial realm. In refusing the distinction between machine- and human-readable forms for glitches, the implied fantasy is that the glitched human-readable form is somehow more pure (closer to the machine-readable form, the digital code) than typical *un*glitched production. Yet, both works are rendered with the same processes, and are simply human-readable forms of a digital work that exhibits unanticipated formal characteristics to their human audience.

Immaterialism is the central feature of how the aura of the digital strips concerns with physical limitations and constraints from our consciousness: compression glitches, (the most common type of glitch encountered), are a transitory, momentary breach in the continuous datastream; we notice that they happen as quickly as we forget they were there. Once the glitch has passed, it vanishes not only from the screen but from concern. Instead of enabling a consideration of the ideological dimensions of these media, the aura of the digital acts to hide them. In this regard, glitch art belongs to the same category of symptom emergent in the arts as James Bridle's new aesthetic and apparent in the translation of it into *style*[19]—both develop from a physicalization of what was/is more commonly purely digital—a realization of immateriality as physicality, revealing a utopian impulse where the reification that stands as proof of an immaterial order both suggests the triumph, and lies beyond the dissolution, of capitalism itself rendered tangible as the glitch. The duality is paralogical; contradictory impulses emerge in digital capitalism as a central part of its expansive procedure, demanding, and then justifying the general deployment of semiotic production as the primary method for wealth generation. This paradox of production without consumption is central to the digital appearing as a magical domain. Both glitch and its related stylistics develop from the same displacement of human agency: in the new aesthetic, this takes the form of production, while in glitch, the attempt is to create an autonomous, critical aesthetic form independent of the human interpretation, reflecting the law of automation's elision of human agency and its replacement by digital, autonomous processes.

3.4

Glitch art, whether the glitches being seen are part of the work, a novel result of some kind of transient technical failure, or a mixture of the two (there is no reason a recorded glitch cannot also be subject to glitches arising from an independent, later technical malfunction) confronts problematics inherent to semiotic facture where an always "perfect," new example of the work in question is made specifically for the moment of encounter. Digital capitalism idealizes data as an immaculate "original," especially obvious when the work encountered is imperfect: the actual human-readable form is a pure product of the digitized samples (datastream) transformed by the decoding protocol; its specifically imperfect character is elided from consciousness by the aura of the digital. However, the errors and imperfections in the digital reproduction tend to disappear from perception precisely because that encounter is secondary to an idealized digital perfection: the audience "tunes out" errors as they occur.

Thus the seeming paradox of an induced glitch as technical failure (i.e., a *desired* glitch whose production was the focus of the technique employed) is a false paradox: it confuses the *intentions* of the machine operator with the *operations* of the machine itself. The idea of materiality (digital or analogue) offers a false potential for critical praxis, thus the recurrent focus on Formalism in challenging the hegemony of capitalist conceptions of media.

The discrete samples that produce digital media are emergent through/hidden by the fragmentary nature of the digital itself: everything "inside" the computer exists as numerically encoded data that when "replayed" for a human audience appears continuous. The glitch makes this apparently perfect "reproduction" become a contingent phenomenon, as glitch artist/theorists Hugh S. Manon and Daniel Temkin noted:

> Glitch art does not "dirty up" a text, but instead undermines its basic structure. Glitch damage is integral, even when its effects manifest at the surface.[20]

The breakdown that glitch imposes on a work (the "text") is totalizing, a failure that in immaterially *generated* work the glitch is a "breach" in the underlying instructions made apparent at the "surface"—the moment of human encounter. Their description reflects the aura of the digital: for them, the datastream is the real form of the work, the human-readable (or physical) form is thus simply an epiphenomenon, inconsequential. A focus on immaterial foundations within the instrumentalist code of any particular glitch prioritizes its generative origin, in the process eliminating the encounter from consideration. By discounting the physical dimensions of the encounter, in favor of the pure error that resides within the code, the aura of information becomes evident.

The paralogical nature of glitches comes into focus when all three variants of technical failure have the same semiotic function and formal appearance within a given work: a glitch can emerge from *either* technical failure or *not*-failure, and still play the *same* role (have the same human-readable form) in the work's interpretation; thus, there is no meaningful difference between a *technical failure* that produced a glitch, a *recorded* version of that same glitch and a *machine designed to produce that same glitch* "live on demand." Yet, for glitches to become critical, the audience's recognition of glitched must allude to a deviant engagement with the anticipated "norm"—whether at the level of datastream, software or hardware (if not all three).

All glitches are a product of the autonomous digital creation (semiotic production) of a given work whose physical characteristics lead to an identification of it as being glitched by the interpreting human audience encountering it. This aspect that limits the conception of glitch is what David Temkin describes in his discussion of glitched jpeg images:

> We can replace all the "DF"s with "1A"s. The result is an image which becomes glitchy in appearance as the image data is altered. The exposure of the code-behind-the-image is part of what helps us recognize this as glitch art. The raw data is exposed for us to hack—this is how many of us began in glitch art, messing with an image data directly in a hex editor, working blindly or referencing glitch tutorials or ancient white papers for file formats. This "broken JPEG" look is one of the most recognizable of glitch aesthetics. It's familiar from Ben Syverson's *Satromizer*, which also alters JPEG data on the byte level, corresponding to the place where one touches the image. When we alter JPEG data this way, changes cascade through a region of the image. JPEG is not just a file format, but an algorithm to compress and decompress image data (actually, the file format is called JPEG JFIF). What gives JPEG corruption its signature look is the way that data for each pixel is not mapped one-to-one to a place in memory but distributed within a matrix, along with the changes we introduce (the "error"). We have not actually "broken" the image in any meaningful sense; we've introduced no structural damage.[21]

The transformation of discrete data within the digital file—his example of replacing all the "DFs" with "1As"—is a transformation of the compressed instruction set that the computer renders into a human readable form; this process is known as databending [Figure 3.4]. These introduced errors produce anomalous results: interruptions of expectation recognizable as the "glitches." While databending is only one method for producing

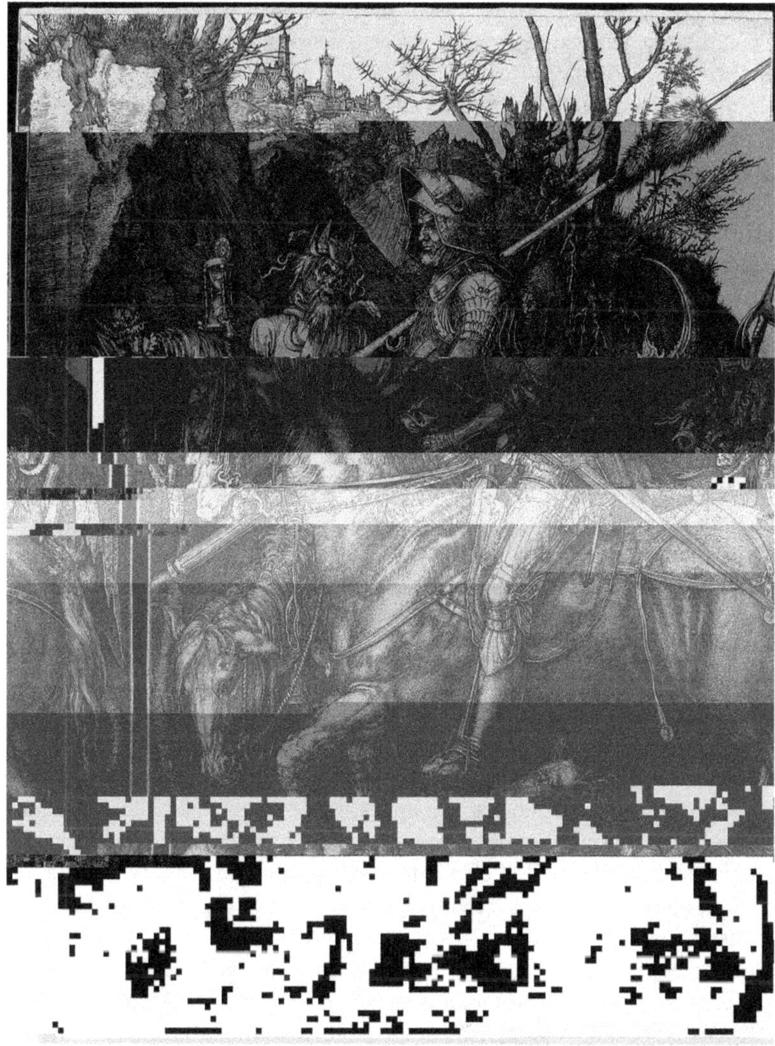

Figure 3.4 Glitched Allegory of the Knight, Death and Durer (2013), by Michael Betancourt

glitches, all methods for glitch share this same formal engagement with the liminal products of what is assumed to be "malfunctioning technology." It is the human engagement—often through their examination and consideration as aesthetic objects—that is the transformative factor which is typically forgotten in looking at and considering digital products of all types because the aura of the digital strips concerns with particular, physical limits from their analysis; the dependence on the human interpreter is always already a physical limitation. The visual results of databending compressed images that Temkin describes appears as a glitch precisely because the results of these changes propagate throughout the jpeg image as the machine renders the instructions into the visible form of the image. These changes assume the form of glitches because they are unanticipated, visible divergences from the expected outcome—even when the original, undatabent image itself is unknown—because the way these changes interrupt the "organic" organization of the image with a different, machine-generated structure formed by how the jpeg compression has resampled/reassembled the image.

This procedural transformation of image data depends on the interventions of a human agent in the production/interpretation of the work. The centrality of this human element becomes apparent in the performance of *Third Hermeneutic.* This encounter between two reproductive technologies mediated by a human performer—Morris himself—who directs and organizes the machines' encounters with each other. The difference between active and passive technologies demonstrates the distinctions between digital computers and the historical analog machines they replaced. The film projectors simply project: the machine runs in a linear fashion, passively unspooling the film; in contrast, the digital machine watches, the DV camera *sees* the screen, and the software actively interprets a response. The performer mediates between these machines, constraining their action, drawing attention to the human element in the construction and generation of the metaphysical *content* of the semiotic abstraction appearing on screen. His role as the consciousness directing the machines affirms the presence of the artist in the work; however, the central elements of this performance render the human central, but *external* to an actively *in*human hermeneutic protocol: the digital itself.

It is the same integral role of human agency that is displaced from consciousness by the aura of the digital. The tendency to look on the human element as secondary (supplemental, but inessential) to the criticality of the work renders this same displacement of the human element as the interpretive process itself, transforming the elision of the human into a foundational assumption; the passivity of the audience in Formalist theory is this same elision of human agency. It surrenders the potential activity of the audience, liquidating it in favor of demiurgic powers for the artist/author. The arguments for an ontological distinction as the essential factor distinguishing glitch from glitch art affirms this same elimination of the audience, dependent on an unidentifiable origin.

The construction of Murata's *Monster Movie* (2005) presents a limited number of shots where a grey, hairy B-movie monster goes on a rampage: the five-minute movie begins with the creature rising out of a dark pool that is seemingly composed from glitches. As this first sequence proceeds, it becomes increasingly colorful, glitched and fluid—at the same time, the original image gradually disappears, leaving behind only the outline of the "monster" as a form that divides the space on screen into "monster" and "not-monster." These images result from a loop repetition of the motion part of the mpeg datastream, leaving out the image data so only the movement remains. This process, datamoshing, produces all the transformations apparent throughout this video—but it also depends on an active process of replacement and reassembly to create the results: the final form of the video requires the actions of Murata. As with Morris's *Third Hermeneutic*, the human role is central to the organization of this glitched video.

The linkage of monster-glitch-dissolution into motion forms that appear throughout *Monster Movie* bring the role of Murata as orchestrator of this technical failure into immediate focus. Without his specific technical involvement, this imagery could not develop in this fashion. It is only because of the removal and repetition of specific parts of the datastream, the "material" basis of the movie, that the monster's rampage becomes possible: it shifts the nature of this rampage from the spectacle of narrative cinema to a spectacle of technical failure rendered continuous. The underlying abstract nature of these images as datastream becomes visible *as* the abstraction seen on screen, but this process is ambiguous: the technical failures of Murata's video is a *novel* spectacle. It does not necessarily engender a critical response or a reflection upon the digital medium *qua* medium, or even glitches *qua* glitches—a critical engagement requires a conscious choice by the audience. The "human element" is necessarily interpretive, capable of reconstituting the technical failure not as interruption, but as the focus and interest in the work; when it does so, the glitch ceases to be error.

Because the hypothetical *perfect reproduction* is reified as "norm" in digital reproduction, the tendency is to consider the identification of a glitch as failure. Yet this construction of glitch-as-failure is possible only because a human interpreter has identified it as at variance from both the *anticipated* imperfections of the immanent work *and* the ideal form. Murata's *Monster Movie* reveals the dependence of glitch on this recognition-interpretation. The suggestion the image is "corrupt" is challenged by the machine's rendering it as a human-readable form. It is by making the fragmentary nature of the underlying medium—the unseen, unencounterable digitized data of the machine-readable form—become a part of how the audience interprets their immanent encounter that the critical dimensions alluded to by theorists such as Menkman, Manon or Temkin become apparent in place of a seemingly continuous media presentation. This context-dependence renders any specific generative origins irrelevant to the critical interpretations that determine a glitch is not simply a momentary technical failure.

Digital technology is instrumental, its coded instructions specifically determinate: the same set of instructions will decode in the same way by the same software every time it is run, whether those instructions themselves contain mistakes (glitches) or not. Thus, an ontological distinction is irrelevant to the consideration of a glitch's meaning in any particular work, because that distinction depends on information that may not be apparent in the glitch itself. This use of ontology to define the glitch does not clarify interpretation, it confuses it: what appears as glitch is a product of the digital machine functioning *properly* (either at the level of hardware or software), but producing results that in a human readable form may appear anomalous—this fact remains true for all glitched works, perhaps most especially in those cases of glitch art where the hardware (or software) has been specifically modified to "short circuit" and generate the glitch form—it is producing what it is *designed* to create. The treatment of glitches as idiosyncratic ruptures with the mechanical functioning of the machine reflects the aura of the digital's mystification of computer technology as a magical realm beyond constraints and human control.

The glitch, and its applications by various digital artists, appears to offer the potential for a rupture in this illusion, a means to access the unseen and invisible realm of the machinic protocol hidden by the apparent perfection of the human-readable form that digital works must take to become phenomenological present. It is this desire to return the dematerialized objects contained by code to the physical work, to make this unknown substrate into a materially present substance that has consistently returned the formal material markers to a central position in aesthetic production. The Modern reduction to these same formal elements reappears as the emergent flattening of differences to the same foundation: the binary encoding of digital technology that is at once totalizing and at the same time transcendent. It substitutes an *ur*-form for the various distinctions of the world, offering up automated semiotic production in place of human labor—in the process extending the fragmentation and alienation of historical industrial labor along its logical path to the elimination of human action entirely.

Notes

1. Walley, Jonathan. "'Not an Image of the Death of Film': Contemporary Expanded Cinema and Experimental Film" in *Expanded Cinema: Art Performance Film*, eds. David Curtis, A.L. Rees, Duncan White and Steven Ball (London: Tate, 2011) p. 244.

2. There are many books covering the history of expanded cinema. See for example, David Curtis, A.L. Rees, Duncan White and Steven Ball. *Expanded Cinema: Art Performance Film* (London: Tate, 2011) or Catherine Elwes. *Installation and the Moving Image* (New York: Wallflower Press, 2015).
3. Weibel, Peter. "The Development of Light Art" in *Light Art from Artificial Light,* eds. Peter Weibel and Gregor Jansen (Karlsruhe: Hatje Kanz, 2006) pp. 190–191.
4. Green, Fitzhugh. *The Film Finds Its Tongue* (New York: The Knickerbocker Press, 1929).
5. "Pure Data—Community Site" *Pure Data* website https://puredata.info/ retrieved July 15, 2015.
6. Russell, Catherine. *Experimental Ethnography: The Work of Film in the Age of Video* (Durham: Duke University Press, 1999) p. 248.
7. Amerika, Mark. *The Museum of Glitch Aesthetics: Featuring the Work of the Artist 2.0* (London, 2012) p. 1.
8. "New Aesthetic" was the title of the blog James Bridle used to collect his materials: new-aesthetic.tumblr.com; he started posting on May 6, 2011 and noted on May 12, 2012 that "The New Aesthetic tumblr is now closed."; he resumed posting new materials on August 20, 2012.
9. Amerika, Mark. *The Museum of Glitch Aesthetics: Featuring the Work of the Artist 2.0* (London, 2012) p. 37.
10. Blackwell, Lewis and David Carson. *The End of Print: The Graphic Design of David Carson* (New York: Chronicle Books, 1995).
11. Menkman, Rosa. "Vernacular of File Formats" in *Network Notebooks 4: The Glitch Moment(um)* (Amsterdam: Institute of Network Cultures, 2011) pp. 17–26.
12. Johnson, C.B. *Modernity without a Project* (New York: Punctum Books, 2015) pp. 4–8; 178.
13. Crow, Thomas. "Unwritten Histories of Conceptual Art" in *Conceptual Art,* eds. Alexander Alberro and Blake Stimson (Cambridge: The MIT Press, 2000) p. 564.
14. Poggioli, Renato. *The Theory of the Avant-garde* (Cambridge: Harvard University Press, 1968).
15. Baudrillard, Jean. *Seduction* (New York: St. Martin's Press, 1990).
16. Crimp, Douglas. *On the Museum's Ruins* (Cambridge: The MIT Press, 1993).
17. Johnson, C.B. *Modernity without a Project* (New York: Punctum Books, 2015) p. 177.
18. Cloninger, Curt. "GltchLnguistx: The Machine in the Ghosts/Static Trapped in the Mouths" in *Glitch reader(ror)*, eds. Nick Briz, Evan Meaney, Rosa Menkman, William Robertson, Jon Satrom and Jessica Westbrook (Unsorted Books, 2011) p. 33.
19. "New Aesthetic" was the title of the blog James Bridle used to collect his materials: new-aesthetic.tumblr.com; he started posting on May 6, 2011 and noted on May 12, 2012 that "The New Aesthetic tumblr is now closed."; he resumed posting new materials on August 20, 2012.
20. Manon, Hugh S. and Daniel Temkin. "Notes on Glitch" in *World Picture 6, WRONG* 2011, http://worldpicturejournal.com/WP_6/Manon.html, par. 29.
21. Temkin, Daniel. "Glitch & Human-Computer Interaction" in *Non-Object Oriented Art*, Vol. 1, No. 1 (January 2014) http://nooart.org/post/73353953758/temkin-glitchhumancomputerinteraction retrieved October 3, 2015.

4 Critical Engagements with Failure

Glitch may serve as an interruption of the aura of the digital's illusion of perfection, at the same time, it is countered by the readily reversible nature of the semiotic: in place of destructive noise, the glitch is more often simply a transient limitation that is quickly elided from consciousness following the aura of the digital: *non-functional (broken) technology is not engaged critically; it is trashed and replaced.*

Glitch becomes political when it creates a stoppage that creates an awareness of that work as a material product, not simply an interruption of functional continuity in the media work, this "awareness" depends on the semiotic role of the glitch making the fragmentary nature of technological presentation visible in its failure. Curt Cloninger's observation in the *Glitch Reader(ror)* that

> The attempt to regulate and filter out the irruptive "noise" and return to the ideal of a pure signal is the same metaphysical/Platonic attempt to downplay the immanent and maintain (the myth of) the pure transcendent. Subverting (literally "deconstructing," in Derrida's original sense) this dichotomous, binary metaphysical system is a radical (root level) "political" act.[1]

The subversion that Cloninger identifies as a political act is one based in rupture experienced by the audience, and does not inhere in the formal material of the work itself. His assertion of a political dimension for glitch (and interruptive/disruptive techniques generally) is apparent in his conceptualization of rupture itself. This interpretation depends on an assumption of glitch in opposition to a singularity, one that is both normative and standard, where any deviation from that norm necessarily carries a political charge; this singularity assumes a passive audience that is not/cannot be engaged with the work in an autonomous fashion. The paradox for glitch as a critical practice (as with political art generally) is the distinction between aesthetic resemblance and reality. However, this "veil of nature"—the semiotic interpretation of glitches as representing technical failure, as in the title sequence for *Halt and Catch Fire*—traps glitches in a position where they cannot present a political meaning; they do not function as stoppages.

The problematic inherent to glitch is not readily resolved through an examination of the instance of the glitch itself; the wild/domestic distinction requires prior knowledge of origins, a generative source that is always hidden by the generative nature of the digital itself: when digital reassembly follows a standardized protocol, the human readable work remains coherent (i.e., matches an anticipated formal 'norm') masking the underlying semiotic procedure responsible for its generation. The indistinguishability of wild/domestic glitches further reinforces this ambivalence for glitch as a class of works, a failing that can be generalized to any critical praxis simultaneously linked to a specific structure; critical interpretations depend on the precise context of a glitch's generation/use. The stoppage results from a violation of established (anticipated) structures within the work—an unanticipated variance from the audience's expectations: the necessary factor in this process is an actively engaged audience that is challenging the work as it proceeds and whose violated expectations produce the glitch. Thus there is no Formalist mode that can present an inherently critical meaning—the emergence of a *specifically* critical meaning depends on active choices made by the audience encountering the work, not the formal design of that work in itself: even the most "critical" glitch may be considered as a simple technical error, dismissing and transforming any criticality as so much "noise" to ignore in the interpretation.

4.1

Digital sampling is a fundamentally distinct phenomenon from continuous experience—it is precisely those aspects of continuity that are lost *in between* the samples that become masked in the encounter with the human-readable form of a digitally generated object. Artist Rosa Menkman's discussion in her book *The Glitch Moment(um)* is typical of how glitches have been theorized following the formal-materialist claims of *film as film*: as a bringing to consciousness of this fragmented (im)materiality of digital media. These claims update the terminology and aesthetic references, but remain within the scope of Gidal's claims for materialist film practice:

> Another example of the *intentional faux-pas*, or glitch art that is in violation of accepted social norms and rules is *Untitled Game* (1996–2001), a combined series of 11 modifications of the first person shooter game (FPS) *Quake 1* by the Dutch/Belgian art duo Jodi. Jodi makes

> subversive glitch art that battles against the hegemonic flows of proprietary media systems. They work to reframe users' or consumers' perception of these systems. The duo's work is often simultaneously politically provocative *and* confusing. This is partly because Jodi never originally prioritized attaching explanations to their work, but also because of the way in which their practice itself overturns generic expectations. They challenge the ideological aspects of proprietary design by misrepresenting existing relationships between specific media functionalities and the aesthetic experiences normally associated with them.[2]

Menkman's argument for a "critical materiality" is the assignment of a critical function to the *glitch qua glitch.* In her argument, the glitched game produced by Jodi achieves a critical position through a formal manipulation of the *functionality* of the work in question mediated by the glitches which are her primary interest in the work. The shift from a game that can be played to one that cannot is a direct effect of how the technology has been "broken." By transforming a functional video game into a dysfunctional (non-functional) version, *Untitled Game* acts against the conventional bourgeois functionalization of the video game; thus, in Menkman's discussion, the work is critical. However, it is the rupture with the *normal* function of the work—its nature *qua* game—and not the glitching *per se* that results in this critical potential. It is the violation of accepted social norms and rules" that is the significant part of this work, not the means employed to achieve that result.

Glitches are thus incidental to the critical dimensions of Jodi's *Untitled Game*: by transforming the function (use value) into dysfunction (glitch) it becomes critical, *not* through a self-referential use of the "materials" of digital media which an "intentional faux-pas" implies. The glitch is not the point here, it is the inability to play the game in the typical, established fashion that produces its critical dimensions—the particulars of the failure in relation to its use, not the formal device of introducing glitches. It is worth remembering that *Untitled Game* is a modification of a relatively low-resolution graphics-driven game, *Quake 1,* released by id Software in 1996, so while the particular failures are essential to the non-productive dimensions of *Untitled Game,* their significance depends on *how* they break the game for the player (audience) not the transformation of the graphics in particular. Menkman's implication is that there is a physical, self-evident distinction between everyday technological failure and the technological failure employed in an art work. It consistently returns to an inherently critical formulation of glitch dependent on an *a priori* distinction between a real and unreal glitch that transcends the actual form either might take. However, there is no consideration of the audience's role in the recognition Menkman describes:

> At the same time, however, many works of glitch art have developed into archetypes and even stereotypical models, and some artists do not focus on the post-procedural dialectics and complexity of glitch at all. They skip the process of creation through destruction of a flow and focus only, directly, on the creation of new formal designs for glitch, either by creating the final imagistic (or sonic) product, or by developing shortcuts to recreate the latest-circulated glitch reformation.[3]

Menkman's "post-procedural dialectics" are problematic. Her discussion simultaneously suggests an argument for an exclusively performative conception of glitch (i.e., glitch as part of a limited and constrained performance created/by an artist) and, at the same time, a rejection of such performative dimensions entirely. Employing a distinction based on the source (a metaphysical claim not necessarily apparent in the work itself) to describe these glitch variants poses logical problems: this contradiction appears clearly when the underlying *performative* nature of all digital media is acknowledged—that every digital work is specifically produced "live" at the moment of encounter. A shift to emphasize *audience interpretation* resolves the problematics of this link between generation-reception by eliminating the importance of this generative source from the consideration of audience interpretation of the given work.

Throughout the twentieth century, the avant-garde's attempts to integrate art into the reality of everyday life can also be seen in reverse—as the taking of everyday life and integrating it into art. The former process creates militancy; the latter, the flaneur, the voyeur, the tourist, as artist/theorist Peter Halley noted in his discussion of transgression:

> Positing no reality beyond the codes, the avant-garde has ignored death as but an invention of language. The avant-garde pursues the idea that in order to revitalize the codes, the mechanism of the codes must be transgressed. It proposed that the moment when this occurred offered a moment of life in the death-like landscape post-symbolic world. From Courbet to the Second World War, this is the paradigm of avant-garde activity, this pursuit of the living moment against the omnipresence of death. [. . .] the post-war artists lost the ability to engage in spontaneous acts of transgression. [. . .] The Abstract Expressionist artists and their supporters consciously sought to create the impression of avant-garde activity by writing letters of protest, staging demonstrations, and

> supporting non-Western art, all with the awareness that these activities conformed to the model of European transgressive practice. Transgression becomes a media event.[4]

Transgression (the disruptive processes and procedures emergent from the opposition of meaning::ambiguity in Halley's framework) in the historical avant-gardes is the source of their "criticality." They exist in direct relationship to earlier conceptions of both Formalist media and a passive audience that is subservient to a network of semiotic codes that constrain and determine their potential engagements *a priori* to their encounter. Any assault upon these established codes is an attack on established semiotic processes employed by humans in ordering their interpretations: ambiguity and meaning are essentially exclusive procedures; paralogy creates a meta-stable realm of shifting signification. The challenge that "glitch" poses is the ways that it may disrupt this ordering process; however, this creating-disarray by glitches depends on them being acknowledged as present in the work—they must first be acknowledged as significant before they can disrupt those semiotic protocols that produce meaning. The simple appearance of a glitch in a work—transient failure—does not disrupt these protocols, making its elision from consciousness (following the aura of the digital) reflective of its *lack* of disruption.

The paradox of this meaning::ambiguity opposition emerges from the role and significance of paralogy. While meaningful statements require a discursive structure where ambiguity is radically reduced, the meaningful statements of art are those where the ambiguity (or, more accurately, multi-valence) plays the strongest role. This dynamic interplay requires intelligent comprehension of the ambiguities themselves—the capacity to produce and distinguish between meanings, functions that the unintelligent process of digital semiosis does not have. It is through the production of multivalent forms—an action specific to human intelligence—recognizing several potential meanings simultaneously emergent in a work, sometimes at differing "levels" of interpretation that is the play of meaning::ambiguity enables through an instability of interpretations. Thus the distinction between the autonomous semiosis of the unintelligent digital machine and the directed intelligence of human comprehension is absolute; assigning the critical functions to glitch as a disruption of digital codes is to mistake the autonomous action of a device for a human activity. The digital necessarily employs a static semiotic system, different in character from human interpretations. For digital machines, the glitch is *not* aberrant because it results from normative function; with a digital system, the semiotic order it has been built to enact necessarily reifies that ordering as the *only* order possible. The machine follows the protocols it has been designed to follow; the glitch, when it appears is not a sign of the machine breaking down, but continuing to function, but with a set of instructions that are aberrant.

The glitches appearing in video *zijkfijergijok* (2002) by the artist collective reMI (Renate Oblak and Michael Pinter) create a pulsating, rhythmic montage of still images whose fragmented structures defy coherent interpretation. Accompanied by a soundtrack of blips and beeps, the bands of glitched imagery flow up the black screen. As with *Digital TV Dinner*, there are fragments of recognizable text, *incipio lamentatio* (Latin for "begin lamentation") that remain almost illegible even as it flickers over the screen [Figure 4.1]. The de/coherence of this glitch structure draws attention to its specific unintelligibility. The rhythmic pulsing of these image/texts invites attempts to decipher it: these attempts are thwarted at the start by the glitched nature of the imagery, but as *zijkfijergijok* develops, the repetitions and loops gradually start building up a coherence as the glitches become normalized as the form of the piece and the image begins to stabilize around partial and fragmented stills showing what appear to be pages from antique Christian texts.

Figure 4.1 Text reading "Begin Lamentation" from *zijkfijergijok* (2002), by the artist collective reMI (Renate Oblak and Michael Pinter)

The recognizable and coherent images that gradually dominate *zijkfijergijok* have what Christian Höller described as an apocalyptic character in the Light Cone catalog entry advertising the video's rental:

> These fragments of knowledge passed down through the ages are just good enough or sufficiently charged that they are suitable for the great revelation in pixel form: abruptly and harshly flickering graphic patterns with piercingly overmodulated »microprocessed» scratch sounds that mercilessly tear everything projected above and below them along into the digital hell.[5]

This connection of glitches to a religious text where the "as above, so below" appears on screen as the rupture in the imagery itself—half the screen is glitched, imagistic, the other half, abyss, empty suggests an alchemy of transformation and translation where the destruction of the imagery is both a symbolic erasure and a metaphoric parting of the veil. What this glitched video reveals through this complex structure is its own failure to be autonomous—the digital procedures acting on these still pictures (re)animate them as they are consumed by the destructive process of sampling essential to the digital. This work assumes a political character through this connection of the glitch to already established symbols (the fragmentary lamentations that appear throughout the video) which it then acts to enhance and highlight: the glitch ceases to be a *technical failure* and instead becomes a metaphoric seeing behind—the blackness of the screen is both an abyss and wall (the reality of the screen as a physical presence). This relationship shifts the nature of the glitch towards the same historical/traditional understanding of the screen-as-window that was the referent for the religious imagery that appears, fragmented, over its surface. The linkage of these abstract forms with the specific mimetic conception of the broken, distorted imagery it shows reveals the limitations of the glitch procedure; *zijkfijergijok* offers a critical view of both the glitches and the imagery it presents *via* the resuscitation of this earlier conception of the image-as-window, a window that is subject to opacity, breakdowns and where meaning always devolves into a semiotic relationship with earlier knowledge and past experience.

4.2

In the title sequence created by designer Patrick Clair for the TV program *Halt and Catch Fire* (2014), the identification of the non-glitched images as glitch and their naturalization as signifiers of technical failure is a *narrative* function of the title sequence's organization. It clarifies the role and importance of past experience in both the comprehension of glitch and the production of critical meanings. This imagery imitates glitch acting as material for commercially standard digital animation and compositing, as Raul Marks, the animator who created these images notes:

> I actually used a very simple Photoshop process to "digitize" the characters' faces. This was as simple as making a rectangular selection on a facial region and then hitting "average" to flatten out the color. Done bit-by-bit over an entire image, you're left with an interesting facial approximation. I get a kick out of it because it's such a simple method but with a great outcome—just takes patience![6]

These graphic distortions of actors' faces resemble the blocky, digitally fragmented structures of glitch imagery [Figure 4.2]. Their similarity to databent imagery is precisely the point: they function metonymically as emblems for the digital breakdown the show's title describes: "hcf" is a term for hardware failure in early computing where the machinery would overheat, stop working and (literally) catch on fire. The design of this title follows a continuous movement of a white "signal" traversing a space filled with a mixture of black and highly saturated red/magenta blocks—the noise created by glitches—to finally reach a climactic point where that white signal activates a sequence of yellow bands arranged in layers. The camera movement and editing emphasize the connections between this action and the activation of a square that represents a silicon chip. The apparent "recuperation" of critical practices this commercial use has for glitch is only problematic if the

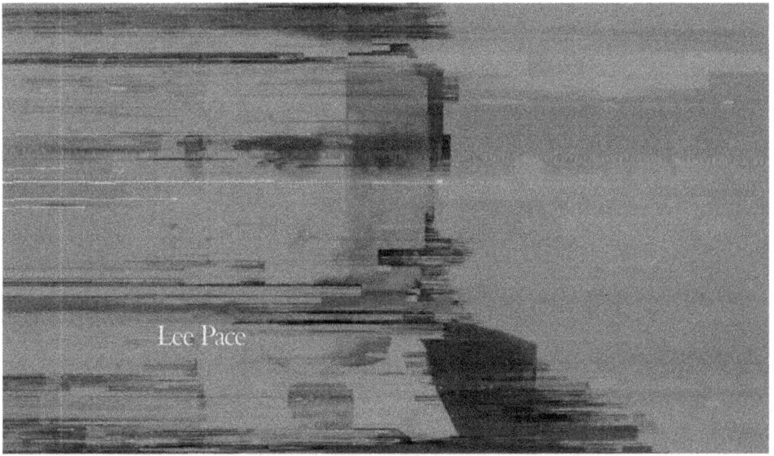

Figure 4.2 Raul Marks, human face from *Halt and Catch Fire* (2014)

glitch is accepted as a metaphysical signifier of critical meaning; the connections between animation, digital blocks and noise elements serve to render this erratic space *natural* as a depiction of a glitchy, virtual space—thus while audiences might identify these images as glitched, their significance is precisely the naturalization of these images as signifiers of/for technical failure. It illustrates the problematic aspects of assuming that a visual form such as glitch has a particular symbolic valence as inherently critical; this title sequence reveals that assumption to be false.

Everything in the *Halt and Catch Fire* title sequence serves to reiterate this singular conception of the digital: as a glitch space populated by aberrant fields of noise through which signal travels as a pure force of action. The design renders the productive action of the digital as an overcoming of glitch and noise to achieve functionality—the productive action reified in this way becomes a spectacle of digital materiality. Aesthetic semblance created by this title design renders the space of digitality as the "natural appearance" of technical failure, thus rendering its glitch portraits into signifiers of technical errors, the pixelated space of this design into a natural depiction of an abstract information space. While these forms are *not* the result of a technical failure, their role in this work is to *represent* those failures, making its consideration relevant to this analysis. The organization of the entire sequence acts to naturalize these errors as the material of digital itself. The title begins entirely with a field of squares in various hues of red and magenta, with a variety of white blocks with streak-trials moving from left to right. It is a physical space, a realm where the digital assumes a distinctly substantive form: when these white streaks encounter a transition between the red space and a darker, black space, one of them *literally* bursts through, with a small flurry of blocks around the point of transition, digital "sparks" as it moves through a barrier [Figure 4.3]. The background shifts between these abstract spaces and spaces that are clearly representational in nature: images of the cast appear out of and decay into this haze of red squares, while the black space is aligned with the interior of a human-outline [Figure 4.4]. Transitions appear as these white ray-streaks encounter squares that on contact burst into animated life, evoking computer chips and microprocessor circuits. This series of connections between actor-human forms and square/grid animations reiterates the connections between these spaces and the abstract imagination throughout the design: it is an imaginary space rendered tangible as an aesthetic semblance of the immaterial digital transformed into the concrete, tangible form of the glitch. This process of linkage and literalization serves to project this materiality beyond the realm of the physical into an imaginary, illusory space, thus neutralizing its disruptive affect and potential as a technical failure. The movement between commercial forms and art forms, a porous and readily transgressed

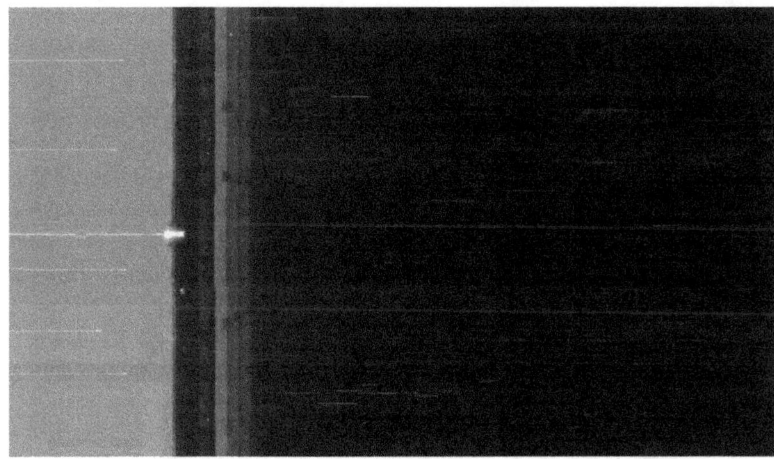

Figure 4.3 Crossing the barrier from *Halt and Catch Fire* (2014)

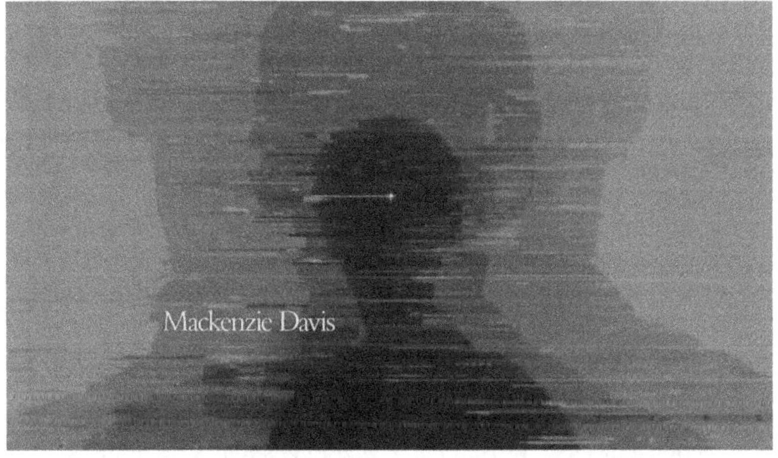

Figure 4.4 Human outline figure from *Halt and Catch Fire* (2014)

boundary according to Tom Sherman's history of video processing tools, is a conceptual shift from "the open-ended, full spectrum video synthesizer as a device with a set of pre-determined 'vision circuits,' pre-set filters for generating art styles through the controlled manipulation and distortion of straight, representational video material."[7] *Halt and Catch Fire* demonstrates this neutralizing of disruptive potentials: the glitch becomes an appropriate *image* whose semiotic function is to designate/represent the idea *technical failure*.

The reappearance of an underlying digital material whose assembly creates the perfect surface can also be understood in terms of a rupture in that work's functionality—in their argument the glitch is a break in continuity *only* if the audience is passive in relation to the work they encounter; however, as Umberto Eco has noted, "It is evident that even the most banal narrative product allows the reader to become by an autonomous decision a critical reader."[8] The assumption that the audience is passive is one this is *not* how audiences engage media: to assume a passive audience mistakes physical immobility for a lack of mental activity.

The *un*critical meaning of *Halt and Catch Fire* and the criticality of *zijkfijergijok* both result from the same process of recognition and interpretation. The morphology and structure of glitches within the differing context of a commercial title sequence versus the art video contributes to the identification of one work as critical and the other as not, as artists Hugh Manon and Daniel Temkin describe in the emergence of critical meaning for glitches:

> Paul Virilio is often cited in discussions of glitch art; however we need to be clear that glitch art is most often not, strictly speaking, an effort to "[p]enetrate the machine, explode it from the inside, dismantle the system to appropriate it." (Sylvère Lotringer and Paul Virilio, *The Accident of Art* (New York: Semiotext(e), 2005), 74.) Real sabotage cannot be undone. Indeed any instance of real sabotage risks spinning out of control to the point of harming the saboteur. In this way, the prevalence of the undo function in glitch practice renders it a kind of pseudo-sabotage. This is not to say that the resultant file—publicly exhibited in some venue—does not disturb, vex, or interrupt the flow of its beholder, and thus work to "dismantle the system." Indeed, despite its simulation of sabotage, glitch art nonetheless loudly announces the hegemony of digital representation and the passivity of its subjects.[9]

The uncritical meaning of *Halt and Catch Fire* is thus a result of its naturalization of this glitch-appearing imagery as a signifier *for* the technical failures, effectively neutering any disruptive potentials they might otherwise have. It returns these potential glitches to the realm of "bourgeois functionalization" understood here as the difference between a pseudo-sabotage and a real-sabotage, determined not by the nature of the glitch, but by its interpretive role in the work. The foundations for this neutralizing is the aura of the digital's claims of the digital as a perfect, immaterial, other-world remote from the constraints and material limitations of physicality. Digital production is the autonomous action of a machine, rather than the particular labor of a human: the difference between the anticipated form and the one produced suggests (and is understood as) a discrepancy between incoding and decoding, rather than as an event emergent from human action; this issue is both immediately obvious and well known when considering both sampled data and the secondary use of compression algorithms in digital technology.

4.3

The literal, immanent decay of these physical materials provides a parallel to the staged and artificial decay of imagery in *Halt and Catch Fire* that illuminates the semiotic function which is determinant of critical meaning. Bill Morrison's feature *Decasia* (2002), composed from found footage—decayed and decaying motion picture films—premiered in Switzerland in 2001 accompanied by a symphony by Michael Gordon.[10] When seen as a digital video, it raises questions about the origins of its film glitches—while they are physical, they could also be the product of digital simulation, an uncertainty that challenges any formal reading of medium-specificity. This extended meditation on actual, physical decay of historical film was made using the same approach to archival materials apparent in his later films *Light is Calling* (2003) and *The Mesmerist* (2003). The transformations imposed by decay on the live action footage become an integral part of the narrative space shown on screen; these glitches are naturalized and contained by the montage, yet produce a critical work precisely because these physical changes are determinant of the *new* motion picture.

Decasia is formed from archival footage in the process of disintegration: it is decayed, but also decaying, a work made from imagery that is rapidly disappearing. These glitches are more than mere scratches or dirt, they are integral ruptures within the apparent continuity of the image, not simply destroying the imagery, but innately transforming it into something entirely different. The "state of decay" shown in this footage is cause for concern [Figure 4.5]. It demonstrates the very real process of disintegration that our collective moving image heritage is experiencing. It is *entropy*, that inexorable movement towards decay. The realization of this physical law in the nineteenth century was a point of existential concern, a fundamental dread that literally suffuses Morrison's film. *Decasia* is made from the disintegrating and distorted imagery of early nitrate films. This historical footage shows scenes from around the world, but not all of the material on screen is so old; however, it is all presented in the same black and white, giving it all a uniform character even when some decayed shots are unquestionably less antique than others.

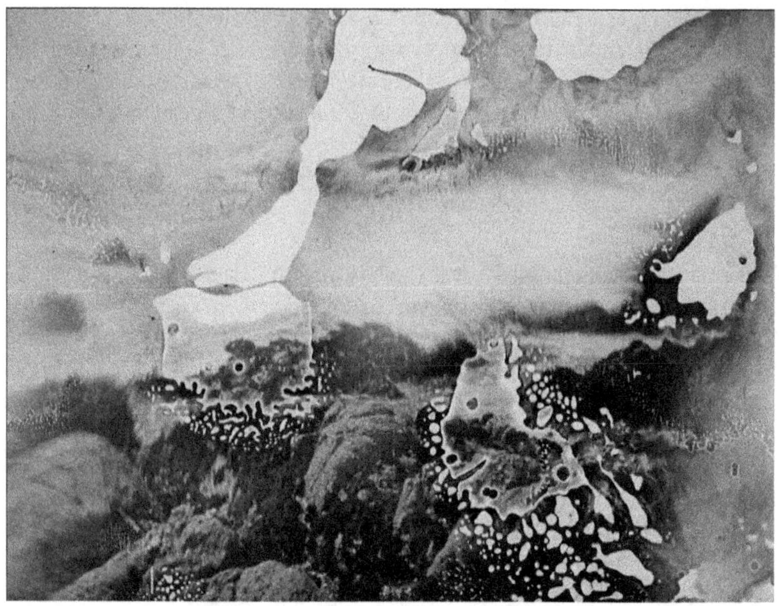

Figure 4.5 Film decay from *Decasia* (2002), by Bill Morrison

Morrison's use of this found footage is distinct from other experimental film makers such as Bruce Conner or Joseph Cornell in the way that his editing of these sequences results in a sense of their *documentary* reality—that what is shown is irreducibly real—bringing the documentary effect of *Decasia* much closer to Dziga Vertov's 1929 *Man with the Movie Camera* than to Connor's 1958 collage film *A Movie*. The references to the film production process at the start (and reappearing throughout) in both Vertov's film and Morrison's *Decasia* serve to remind the viewer that what they are watching is *film*. It brings the productive aspects of cinematic labor into consciousness, rendering the means of production part of the meaning of the work. This inclusion establishes the critical meaning for the glitches as other than (in excess to) their narrative and stylistic roles: they become a signifier not only for time and decay, but for the same processes active in the *real* world beyond the film narrative. What *Decasia* presents is taken from the real world: this is a work "of reality" rather than "of fiction." It is this aspect of *Decasia* that has been carefully considered by film historian Michele Pierson's 2009 *Cinema Journal* article "Avant-Garde Re-Enactment: *World Mirror Cinema, Decasia,* and *The Heart of the World.*" In her concluding remarks, she observes that *Decasia* suggests a dehumanized perspective on humanity and the natural world, yet does not develop this into a full interpretation of the film.[11] What unites the materials of *Decasia* is the presentation of a *world* on film that is undergoing fragmentation, dissolution, decay—most visibly in the voids that have opened up in some of the first shots: a gaping white void obliterates the visible world, transforming what is onscreen into an abstract field of pulsating whites and stringy, black strips. Gradually the shot progresses and it becomes clear what we are seeing is a real world, an interior perhaps in Japan, that no longer exists. In watching these scenes, it quickly becomes apparent that those people who inhabit this filmed world are mere shadows, both metaphorically and literally fragile beings whose mere existence is under a constant threat of collapse. Throughout this opening section, before and during the titles, the nature of the montage becomes apparent: it is neither just a collection of glitches, nor a documentary on the need for film preservation, but a carefully structured portrait of a world *in* decay, a world that is literally disintegrating as we see it revealed on screen. Within the space of this montage, the role of cinema—motion pictures—is as both a material preservation against things falling apart and the revelation of this universal, systemic decay.

That the majority of this filmed material is simultaneously historical—early films produced on nitrate stock—and documentary in effect is not accidental: even though some of these shots were clearly originally part of some type of fictional narrative, they assume a documentary character when they are removed from their original context, often isolated as single shots. What their glitches reveal returns our consideration to a basic fact about so many films: they are recordings made with a camera of people who actually lived. That the places and things we see in many of these scenes often have a familiar quality (as in Figure 4.6, where Greeks in native costume perform their traditional dances on the Acropolis in Athens, the Erechtheion in the background) works to ground the more clearly fictional scenes in their profilmic reality of actors, sets—once living people being preserved on film. The continuous assertion of reality for this world held within these shots brings the decay into progressively sharper focus. What initially appears to simply be a surface affect (style), not a feature of this world, rapidly begins to suggest otherwise: these glitches twist faces, burn bodies and cut holes in the world are not just the effect of time on nitrate film stock, but are instead an inherent feature of the world itself, rupturing the imaginary divide between then and now. The historical distance of Bazin's realism collapses: the ravages of time are also the decay inherent in the world it depicts, our world that produced these images. It is an unavoidable consequence of being a living person, not just at the start of the twentieth century but today as well.

Decasia is a horror film in which the horror it presents as the corruption imposed by time on what people create is also an unavoidable part of the world we live within. (Similar themes of horror run throughout Morrison's other films made from decaying archival stock footage.) What is frightening about *Decasia* is not only the destruction of these old films, but the implication and reminder that this destruction is not contained (safely) within the art object. It is an invocation of the same terror felt in the nineteenth century with the realization of what entropy—the second law of thermodynamics that states everything will tend towards the lowest energy state—really means: that things fall apart, the center cannot hold, the world will end, not with a bang but a whimper. This horrific poetry brings us into a contemplation of just how small humans really are, how we inhabit an inhuman, alienating and indiscriminately hostile universe where all our endeavors will ultimately come to dust. This terror is the existential core of *Decasia*, and its encounter is always just beneath the surface, guiding the montage and reflected in the continuously descending notes of the mantra-like score. This discovery mirrors what Enlightenment philosopher Edmond Burke called the "sublime" in his book *A Philosophical Inquiry into the Origins of Our Ideas of the Sublime and Beautiful* (1757). It is our encounter with this vast, terrifying force we have lived with our entire life that only becomes apparent through the intervention—mediation—of art:

> Whatever is fitted in any sort to excite the ideas of pain and danger, that is to say, whatever is in any sort terrible, or is conversant about terrible objects, or operates in a manner analogous to terror, is a source of the sublime [. . .] it easily follows, from what we have just said, that whatever is fitted to produce such a tension must be productive of a passion similar to terror, and consequently must be a source of the sublime, though it should have no idea of danger connected with it.[12]

Burke's understanding of the sublime is two-fold. The sensation of terror is central to it, but it is a terror separated from immanent threat or danger. Yet, it is not enough that the sublime provoke terror since there are many things capable of eliciting such a feeling; nor is it enough that the sublime is an encounter with something vastly larger and more powerful than ourselves—these are his fundamental conditions, but it is their interaction that creates the sense of the sublime and offers the critical meaning this film proposes for these glitches. Within *Decasia* this terror arises precisely from the relationship between these signs of the decay and the world shown with this film: the two are intrinsically linked, not just at the formal level of image-material support, but diegetically, and it is the apparent interaction by the people seen in the film and presence of the glitches within their world that is the source of the terror: it collapses the distinctions normally present

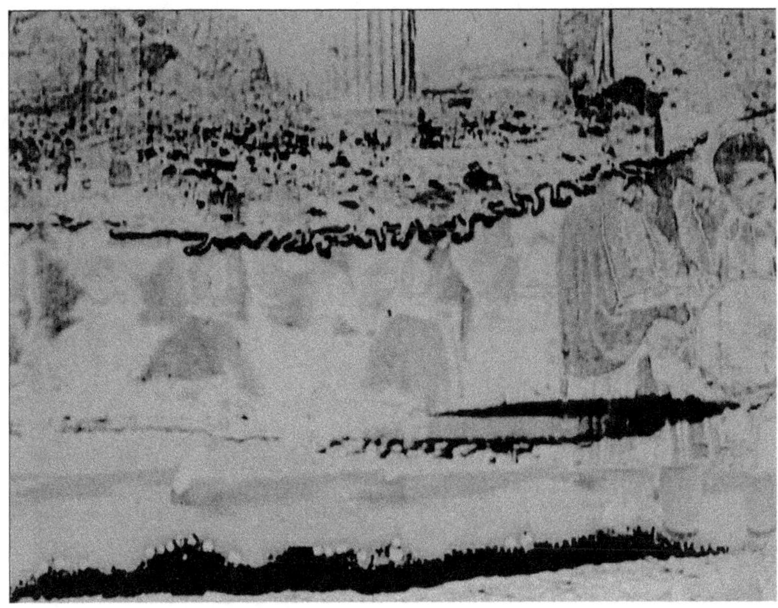

Figure 4.6 Still from *Decasia* (2002), by Bill Morrison

in theatrical works between the fictional world (diegesis) and the realm that lies outside of it. This shifting of relations depends on the documentary character that all filmed images have—they are recordings of actions—even when (perhaps especially when) they are creating a fictional world. It is the rupture of this mental barrier that separates the formal, fictional and documentary dimensions of these shots that develops the terrible recognition that the world being shown is the world we inhabit. This linkage appears rapidly, within the first few minutes of the film, and is one that continuously resurfaces within the montage as the decay has an unstable relationship to what we see on screen—in one shot it is the physical collapse of the celluloid itself [Figure 4.6], in the next it enters into the narrative space, interacting with the people shown [Figure 4.7]. What happens in these encounters is a transformation of consciousness where the terror and vastness of the entropic universe becomes the foundation for a sense of more than just these two feelings: it is this emergent, third experience that is Burke's sublime and is what links the sublime to the uncanny. Their difference lies with the positivity or negativity of the resulting sensation: the sublime is transcendent in nature; the uncanny is materialist.

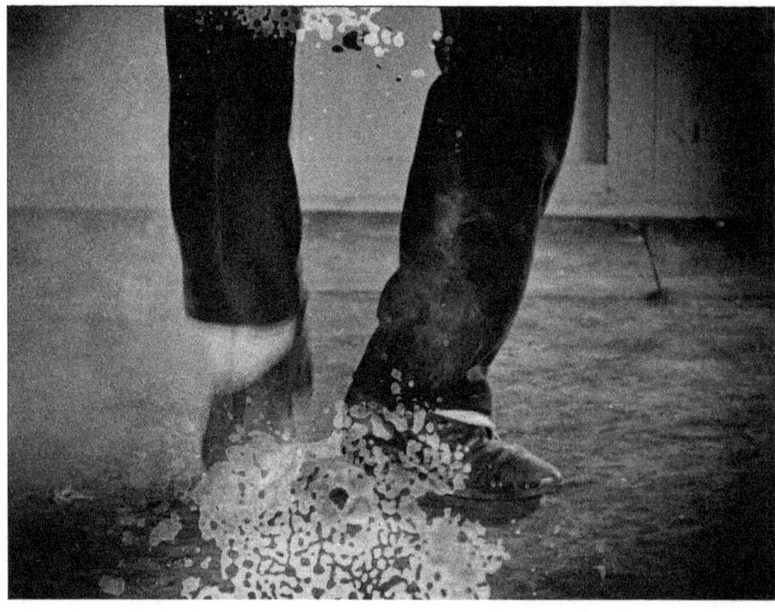

Figure 4.7 Man apparently interacting with the visual results of decay in *Decasia* (2002), by Bill Morrison

However, the sublime dimensions of Morrison's film, like the existential terror it invokes, are tempered by the negentropic actions of the people we see within the film. The glitches are contained and challenged by the action shown in this narrative, creating a dynamic interaction between critical meaning and their narrative function that links this experimental film to the protocols and methods of commercial media—the same protocols that *Halt and Catch Fire* deploys. The differences of duration—*Decasia* is a feature length film and *Halt and Catch Fire* is a title sequence—are irrelevant to their meanings. The different semiotic roles for their apparent glitches are not a function of their material origins, but a demonstration of the importance of *how* they are organized within the work itself. This issue does not depend on dialectics or on any particular ideological framework to support its criticality.

Decasia is organized as visual music into movements whose names are contained in the liner notes and menus of its DVD release, reinforcing the documentary montage of life inside an entropic universe: (1) creation; (2) civilization; (3) conundrum; (4) disintegration and rebirth. The boundary between one and another is implicit in the development of the film, but not explicitly marked within its progress. Musical changes rather than intertitles announce each section's beginning; materials repeat throughout the film, and no section is really independent of the others. As a sequence of descriptions for the structure of the resulting montage film, what they reveal is the circular nature of the whole: it concludes with many of the same images that appeared in the beginning, but in reverse. The line of camels crossing a chaotic desert of real decay from right to left at the start, appear a second time, returning across this same desert—still seething with rot and decay—crossing from left to right, a return to their origin point. The symmetrical organization of the start and finish suggests the cycle these chapter headings allude to and that is responsible for the film's existence. The transformation of pristine image to decay, the concomitant loss of coherence that becomes a new organizing principle for all this footage as it takes shape in an entirely *new* construction. Destruction—rebirth becomes a cycle linked to the material nature of the source material, and implicit in its (re)production as an entirely new motion picture, one that is independent of these initial sources.

While glitches dominate *Decasia,* at the same time, it is a film filled with images of spinning and rotating things linked not to destruction, but to maintenance. These images start at the very beginning (and are repeated at the very end) with the motion picture of a dervish rotating in place [Figure 4.8]. It

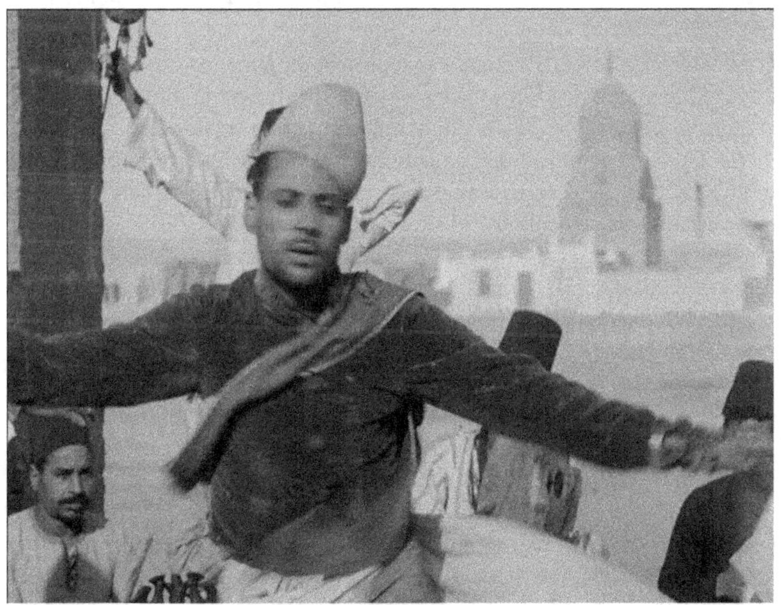

Figure 4.8 Spinning dervish from *Decasia* (2002), by Bill Morrison

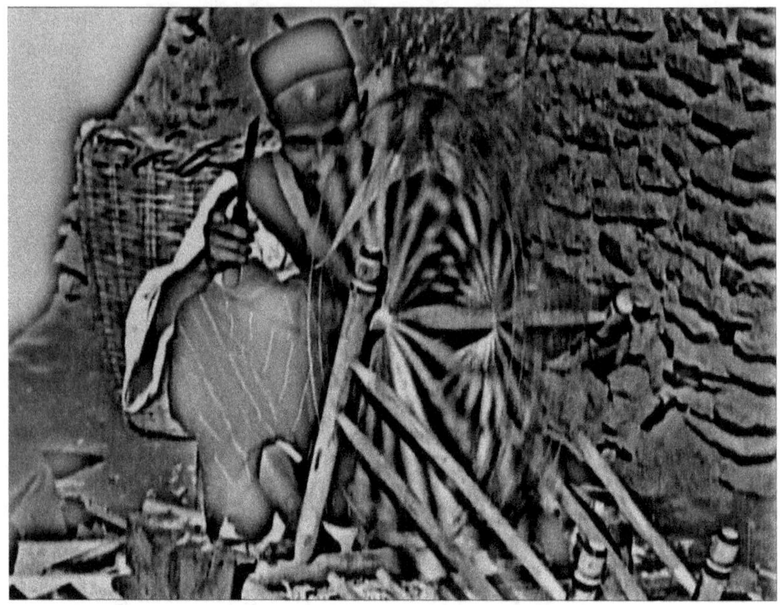

Figure 4.9 Solarized image of weavers from *Decasia* (2002), by Bill Morrison

is this *spinning* action that comes to represent the negation (however temporary) of this decay, and is the means by which the people of this world on film attempt to contain the degradation and destruction that seethes all around them. The connection of spinning to preservation is not a mere accident: motion picture films themselves unspool from reels that closely resemble the other spinning wheels and other devices that appear at the end of the first movement. In the second section, "civilization," the first spinning image is accompanied by a shift in music from a descending glissando of notes to a stable, high pitched oscillation that mirrors the spinning wheel's motions. It is not simply that the world is decaying and we live within this continuous degradation, but that we engage it on many levels. Unlike the earlier scenes of a world coming apart—of spots, holes and distortions threatening to overwhelm the image, this shot is remarkably stable [Figure 4.9]. The figures glow with the Sabatier effect, solarized, burning but not consumed.

This shot is countered by others where the decay appears to be confined, contained, not so much damage to the film, but a feature of the photographic world shown on screen: the decay is integral, rather than superficial [Figure 4.10]. The people on screen seem to interact with it, aware and conscious of the decay's effect. This shift from non-diegetic destruction of the film base to a diegetic element of the screen-space is what renders the terrors

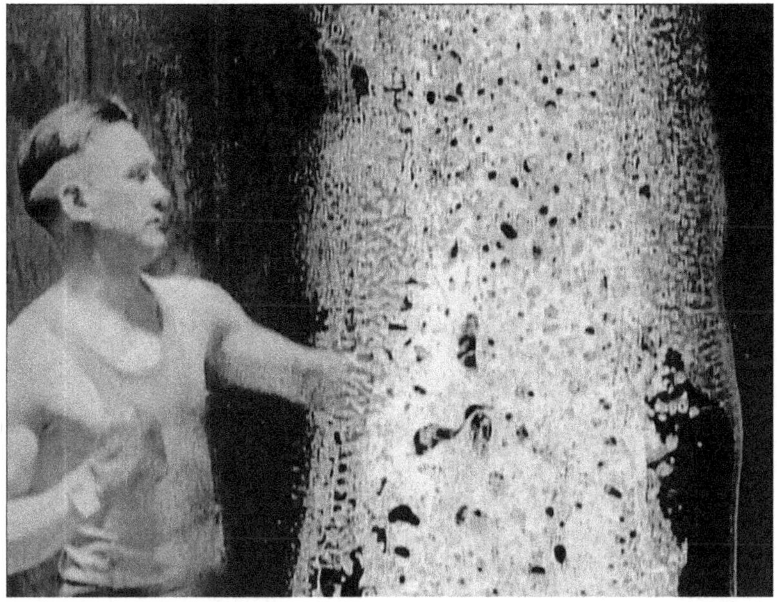

Figure 4.10 Man boxing with film decay from *Decasia* (2002), by Bill Morrison

specific to *Decasia.* What we see on screen is not only a record of the current state of decay in archival film—it is a world that is *in* decay, internally, continuously. This film presents the terror felt when the nineteenth century first realized the implications of the scientific theory of entropy: that the "lowest energy state" for the complex system that is the universe itself is death; things fall apart; the center cannot hold. This discovery of entropy is what appears in *Decasia*—the revelation that the world *on* film as much as the world contained *by* film are equally linked to this entropic winding-down. The only force that appears in *Decasia* as a counter to this entropic disintegration is the spinning—dervish, wheel, machine, film reel—a process that does not so much stop the decay as achieve an equilibrium with it. The rotational power of these forms punctuate the sequences showing this world of decayed and decaying matter, the only points where momentary stability becomes possible.

This stability is an illusion; the shifting roles of glitch—as both material signifier of physical decay and breakdown and semiotically within the narrative space as signifier for a world *in* collapse brings glitch back to its paralogic function. *Decasia* employs recognizable and familiar techniques from the materialist film in direct dialogue with the protocols of commercial media, creating a critical meaning that draws attention to the production and destruction of cinema without reference to its capitalist context. It thus provides a model for critical meaning independent of both technology and ideology; it is critical without the restrictions of Modernist Formalism. The semiotic role of technical failure in *Decasia* thus functions politically, but without recourse or reliance on a Marxist dialectic that rejects the mimetic aspects of commercial cinema. Instead, this film employs those codes to challenge their meaning and render their presentation discomfiting, a political statement about precarious reality.

Notes

1. Cloninger, Curt. "GltchLnguistx: The Machine in the Ghosts/Static Trapped in the Mouths" in *Glitch reader(ror)*, eds. Nick Briz, Evan Meaney, Rosa Menkman, William Robertson, Jon Satrom and Jessica Westbrook (Unsorted Books, 2011) p. 35.
2. Menkman, Rosa. *Network Notebooks 4: The Glitch Moment(um)* (Amsterdam: Institute of Network Cultures, 2011) p. 38.
3. Menkman, Rosa. *Network Notebooks 4: The Glitch Moment(um)* (Amsterdam: Institute of Network Cultures, 2011) p. 35.
4. Halley, Peter. "After Art" in *Peter Halley Collected Essays: 1981–1987* (New York: Sonnabend Gallery, 1991) pp. 111–112.
5. Höller, Christian. "zijkfijergijok" http://lightcone.org/en/film-3668-zijkfijergijok, accessed October 13, 2015.
6. "A discussion with Director PATRICK CLAIR and Lead Animator RAOUL MARKS." on *The Art of the Title Sequence* http://www.artofthetitle.com/title/halt-and-catch-fire/, accessed October 12, 2015.
7. Sherman, Tom. "Machine Aesthetics are always Modern" in *The Emergence of Video Processing Tools, Volume 1*, eds. Kathy High, Sherry Miller Hocking, and Mona Jimenez (Chicago: Intellect Books, 2014) p. 91.
8. Eco, Umberto. "Serial Form" in *The Limits of Interpretation* (Bloomington: University of Indiana Press, 1994) p. 92.
9. Manon, Hugh S. and Daniel Temkin. "Notes on Glitch" in *World Picture 6 WRONG* 2011, http://worldpicturejournal.com/WP_6/Manon.html, par. 25.
10. Kehr, Dave. "Symphony of Compositions from Decomposition" in *The New York Times*, December 21, 2012.
11. Pierson, Michele. "Avant-Garde Re-Enactment: *World Mirror Cinema, Decasia*, and *The Heart of the World*" in *Cinema Journal*, Vol. 49, No. 1 (Fall, 2009) pp. 1–19.
12. Burke, Edmund. *A Philosophical Inquiry into the Origins of Our Ideas of the Sublime and Beautiful* Sections Part I, Section VII; Part III, Section V (1756).

Prospects

Critical media depend on critical engagements. Specific ruptures rapidly become assimilated as signifiers within the already established formal language of the medium being glitched: this normalization elides dialogue, resistance and change—it is a procedure mirrored by social assimilation and class aspirations where lower classes mimic the fashions of higher social classes in a process that entails an uncritical adoption of forms and customs.[1] The implicit threat this "passive acceptance" (mimicry) poses is countered by the simultaneous conception of those seeking to assimilate as disengaged "followers," passive in their behaviors. The conception of a passive audience recasts this view of the *active* process required by imitation as a passive acceptance that is incapable of critical or instrumental action—the social function of a passive audience reaffirms traditional class structures. It links the conception of audience as passive with other conceptual structures reinforcing the class distinctions and structural valuations of human labor in capitalism. This social dimension of class and social status is apparent in the traditional conception of audiences as *passive,* acted upon rather than actively engaged; it informs the critique developed by Adorno, assumed by Gidal and implicitly retained by Contemporary glitch theorists. The fixed positions of these relations assure the continuation of this structure; the paralogistic ambivalence of glitch potentially challenges this fixity, suggesting these social and class relations are mutable—and with them the political framework they reify. The entire history of media art can be described as debates about priority for one type of formal/interpretive engagement over another.

The semiotic view of audiences as active, engaged and interpreting the work they encounter opens the scope of uses for glitch to a wide range of discursively contradictory approaches apparent in how the spectator assimilates the apparent failures and glitches of media following what critic Brian

Larkin described as "recoding" in his discussion of media piracy and the informal distribution systems of Nigeria:

> If infrastructures represent attempts to order, regulate, and rationalize society, then breakdowns in their operation, or the rise of provisional and informal infrastructures, highlight the failure of that ordering and the recoding that takes its place.[2]

The failure of one system does not result in a wasteland, abyssal, but rather an emergent replacement—a reorganization of the (dys)functional elements around the precise (dys)function itself—what was a point of failure becomes the central feature of a return-to-normal: hence a *recoding* of the existing order to integrate the failure, assimilating the glitch as the image [Figure 5.1]. The issues of stoppage vanish in this transformative process: glitch ceases to be rupture and becomes instead the *signifier of rupture,* and with this transposition to signification (recoding) is a regeneration of the "norm," reflected by the disappearance of the glitch from consideration as a stoppage of function.

The self-similarity of "real glitch" and "simulated glitch" (domesticated or glitch-alike) demonstrates the contingent nature of how any particular glitch has been employed semiotically within the human-readable form: it is possible to imagine a reversal where the "*un*glitched" serves the same disruptive role in the semantic structure as the glitch—a bringing to consciousness of the process and transformations posed by the work itself—in a recoding of the *already recoded.*

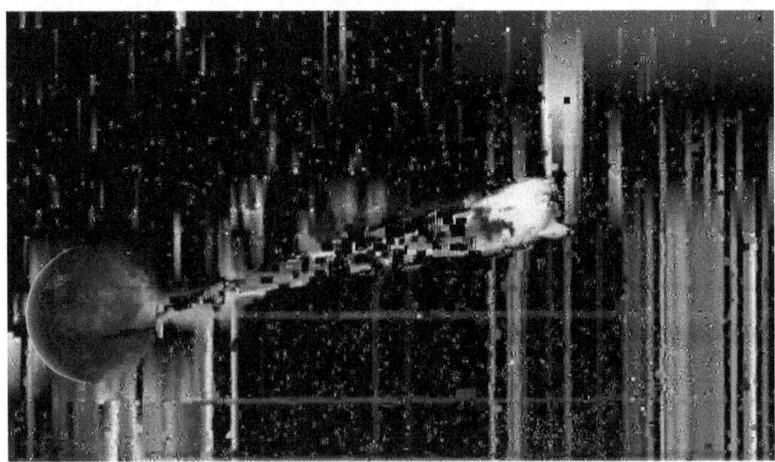

Figure 5.1 Still from *Going Somewhere* (2016), by Michael Betancourt

This process of recoding becomes apparent in the glitch video *zijkfijergijok* as the shift in function from disruption to meaning: as the glitched elements appear throughout this video acting as a consistent device for the fragmentation and interruption of recognizable imagery, their formal role suggests a grammatical function as a semiotic device. The transition from interruption and non-sequitur to signification and grammatic transforms the nature of these glitches fundamentally, assigning them a functional role in the meaning of the work. The semantic role of the glitches in reMI's video is one that depends on their formal appearance and organization *as* glitches—they are what they appear to be. This signification depends on the identification of glitch *qua* glitch—as technical failure—even though it is a technical failure transformed into signifier. The meaning of these glitches is paralogical since they are a medium-specific technical failure: they are ciphers for themselves, at once both technical failure and symbol for that failure.

These transformations are an emergent phenomenon of perception/interpretation and the always already imposed constraints of past experience on that immanent encounter: a glitch *may* provoke an awareness of the materiality of the medium when it is contained in an otherwise *unglitched* work; however, a work composed from glitches poses a radically divergent awareness, one in which the medium itself does not necessarily become physically present, suggesting the emergence of a different mode that is no less normative in its operation. The reversion to norm at the conclusion of *Digital TV Dinner* is a prime example of this *unglitch* functioning critically as a revelation of the productive aspects of the work. The assertion of continuity is a feature of how the digital aura imbues digital works with their specific valence as immaterial, quite apart from whatever physical example may be encountered at any given moment, enabling the discounting of the glitch and technical failure, in a specific elision where they are always conceived as only momentary, a feature only of *this* presentation, thus irrelevant to consideration. The immanent recuperation of technical failure as uncritical signifier has the potential to reverse, becoming a structural revelation of the fallibility and fungibility of the established order; this reversibility is what creates the *un*glitch.

The rupture that stoppages pose for illusions of perfection, transparency and immediacy invites the assumption that glitch is necessarily critical; Caleb Kelly writing in his book *Cracked Media* describes how this entanglement leads to apparent solutions:

> The practice of cracking and breaking playback media folds the flow of production and consumption back on itself. The imagined transparent and passive mediating devices of storage and playback are transformed into generative technologies by practitioners of the crack and break,

> breaking the linear flow of production and consumption. [. . .] Through the destructive act, artists directly question the value of the media itself and the way we have been taught to carefully handle it.[3]

Kelly's analysis remains recognizably within the parameters of established criticality by ignoring the distinction between the audience and the work itself—the mediating role of an audience expecting a "critical work" introduces an element of observer demand into this engagement that is missing from his discussion: if these cracked works challenge the imagined transparency of the playback—an illusion posed by the aura of information—they do not challenge "the way we have been taught to carefully handle it" because this proposition is what vanishes under the illusion that digital media are a metaphysical form independent of the physical world. Digital capitalism functions as a pervasive and interlocking set of assumption-constraints about the relationship between physical production and digital technology. The autonomous generation by the digital system of a *new* object on demand each time we want to access it instantiates a process of elision and rejection of historical and material constraints that the glitch can challenge only sometimes—and only under the very specific conditions discussed earlier in this analysis. The dynamic problem for critical interpretations posed by digital technology reside with their chimerical, Janus-like duality: they are a reification of the same capitalist protocols that they appear to challenge through the illusion of an end to scarcity and limits. Kelly's analysis emphasizes the difficulty of criticism within the network of reflections and mirroring the digital creates.

The transformations effected by glitch art (in fact all re-enactments of the inherently critical claim) depend on the audience recognizing the ritualized critical position posed by the work's morphology and structure as non-function: a recoding of the failure as a signifier for failure. It is a reiteration of how simulated material markers of photo-chemical motion pictures function in commercial feature film production: the appearance of film grain, the imperfections of camera shake and focus, the allegoric appearance of unplanned events witnesses rather than directed—act to assert the material realism of the digitally generated imagery, signifiers that must be added to the digital. These elements are *not* glitches, but their semiotic role as representations of materiality function as symbolic of "film" in the same way that glitches can function as symbolic of digital failure. This understanding of glitches as material demonstration is a recuperation of failure as meaning, the assimilation of technical failure as the superficial marker for the digital damage. Recoding results in a normalization of this superficially disruptive element posed by the glitch—whether its origins lie with technical failure or the domestication of the "glitch-alike." Larkin observes that the resilience of the capitalist system that produces the conceptual and physical infrastructures of media utilizes this human capacity for adaptability:

> The difficulty here is that much of the work on the transformative effects of media on notions of space, time, and perception takes for granted a media system that is smoothly efficient rather than the reality of infrastructural connections that are frequently messy, discontinuous, and poor.[4]

The duality he assumes in media between a seamless, perfectly efficient (digital) media, as opposed to a "messy, discontinuous, and poor" physicality, while perhaps especially obvious in the Nigerian context he describes, is also applicable elsewhere in the world; however, it is the capacity of the audience to ignore these physical traces in the media work that is significant—this disappearance of the noise is the aura of the digital stripping that imperfect physical presentation from consciousness, a rendering transparent of the technological failings (thus, meaningless and non-critical). Distinctions between different media have historically been based upon the materials employed; however, this separation begins to break down when we encounter photography or film, and its difficulty is compounded by the myriad forms and uses the digital computer offers us. Speaking of digital formats such as .mpeg, .mp3 or flash files as separate media in the same way that watercolor, oil paint or bronze are different media, leaves a sense that something vital is missing from this description—not least the fact that the work presented in one format can be fluidly translated into another. The impact that the aura of the digital has on our encounters with all media—whether "perfect" or "imperfect"—undermines the potential of glitch to function disruptively as a breach in the "(im)materiality" of media works. Glitches emerge not from errors but from the audience's *interpretation* of elements within a specific work *as* technical failure—critical engagement does not depend upon the *formal* nature of the art. This capacity is exploited by digital capitalism in its expansion and assimilation of critical challenges. The aura of the digital specifically describes this process of normalization that the stoppage challenges: the problem for critical media is not the creation of stoppages, but the adaptability of the audience to the stoppage itself.

This semiotic model of interpretation is incompatible with the inherently critical mode derived from Adorno's *Aesthetic Theory*—the particulars of any interpretation are contingent not only on the work, but on what and how the encounter with that work develops, a factor Menkman notes in *The Glitch Moment(um)*:

> The post-procedural essence of glitch art is opposed to conservation; the shocking perception and understanding of what a glitch is at one

> point in time cannot be preserved for a future time. The artist tries to somehow demonstrably grasp something that is by nature unstable and ungraspable. Their commitments are to an unconventional utopia of randomness, chance and idyllic disintegrations that are *potentially* critical. [emphasis original][5]

While interpretation is constrained by and focused through the apparent features of any given work, at the same time, it is dependent on past experience and expertise brought to that work: her implication is that the potential for criticality depends on the (momentary) disruption—but then fails to recognize that for functionally-motivated interpretations, the glitch is a stoppage, *not* a point of rupture. It is an interruption that may require action different than a consideration of the actual physical nature of the work itself. Descriptions of this type tends to become reductive: the physical properties of the materials overshadow the relationship between the materials, interpretive procedures or techniques, and the empirically apparent properties of a specific work. This aspect of Formalism becomes the foundation for Gidal's materialist film—the presentation of materiality in the form of grain, frame lines, tape splices, dirt, fingerprints, etc.—are mirrored in the arguments around digital failures as revelations of a digital materiality. Formalist arguments for purity by Gidal as much as in Loos or Greenberg proceed from the conception of materiality as definitional. The critical element for glitch that is the underlying concern of Menkman's argument emerges from *how* the glitch interrupts the *anticipated* flow of a work—its action as stoppage—and the significance of those interruptions when they do appear. Critical meaning is dependent *not* on the glitch itself, but on its role *within* a given work. This slippage and vacillation over the relationship between the Modern and the Contemporary within theorizations of glitch reveals the basic contradiction between the physicality of media that glitch represents, and the audience's interpretive interaction with it.

These problematics of glitch as a politically engaged media practice foreground ruptures and conceptual differences of these theoretical models, demanding an approach that accounts for the role of context, audience adaptation and the recoding of interpretation: this recognition does not eliminate the potential for an engaged media practice—instead, it places an emphasis on the *actual* form of that work. The construction of a work entirely from glitches would then seem to preclude the potential for any critical position, effectively transforming the glitched work into a normative (but still glitched) example of Adorno's "bourgeois functionalism": since criticality is not an inherent property of a work, but a function of how the audience interprets that work, the issue of criticality must instead develop from the particular features of the work, its presentational context, and structured form—to do otherwise would be to reassert an *a priori,* inherently critical position for *all* works of a given class such as glitch art. This difficulty may be a reason why so many discussions attempt to employ an ontological division between "glitch" and "glitch-alike."

The argument for an inherent critical mode is a necessarily false one; a product of contradictions and fallacy. The transformation from functional to non-functional does not render the art object *necessarily* critical. These are issues not isolated to digital art and glitch, but inhere in art generally. Marcel Duchamp, in thinking about the relationship between meaning and form from the perspective of an artist, provides valuable insight into the dynamic relationship between critical approaches and heuristics employed by artists. Understanding the role of Formalism in these parallel constructions requires an acknowledgement of the links between the manipulation of physical materials (morphology) and the relationship their meaning (structure); intellectualization as opposed to encounter. Duchamp's rejection of "retinal art" describes this orientation precisely. His comment that "Painting should not be exclusively visual or retinal. It must interest the gray matter; our appetite for intellectualization"[6] identifies this proposal of intellectualization as semiotic; these are the same central issues for any interpretation of glitches as critical. We interpret the physical aspects of the art object separate from, and independent of, the actual object itself. The contingency and ambivalence of these critical modes reveal the interpretation of work via spectatorship is *not* a passive experience or activity. Marcel Duchamp's ready-made *Fountain* (1917) is a paradigmatic example of how assuming an inherent criticality to the form is to misapprehend the *critical* meaning of the work: it is *not* the non-functional orientation of this urinal that renders the work critical; *it is the installation of a urinal in an art gallery that generates the critical meaning*—a function of its specific exhibition *context*. Because *Fountain* can function as an aesthetic object independent of its utilitarian origins (as urinal) demonstrates the problem it poses for critical meanings. Functional or non-functional, it is the frission of object-versus-context, not the ontologies of the object in isolation that renders its interpretation as a *critical* work. This process includes the recoding of the work as aesthetic, requiring its *functional* transformation via semiosis (contra Adorno), a necessary functional change that glitched works such as *zijkfijergijok* demonstrate. The critical meaning is dependent on interpretation, not its material form as glitch. Instead, the audience for *any* work will dynamically adapt to the semiotic structures *implied* in the construction of any particular work[7]—enabling the recoding of glitch as normative, as the symbolic presentation of technical failure: the revelation of the *medium as such* is only a temporary phenomenon.

Critical interpretations depend on the audience for a work (via established expertise and past experience) recognizing both the glitch—i.e., the acknowledgement that it is a feature of the work rather than a technical failure to ignore—*and* being able to understand the role it has as disruption within the continuous media work—the semiotic role that a *specific* glitch has in determining the meaning of the work compared with other works. Cory Archangel's *Super Mario Clouds* (2002) is structured in similar ways to Jodi's *Untitled Game*—yet the differences are significant. Both works employ appropriated commercial video games altered by the artists to produce different-than-normative results. Where *Untitled Game* mimics the form of a dysfunctional game (unplayable because of seeming malfunction), *Super Mario Clouds* is equally unplayable, but not from visible malfunction, but rather from an *absence* of functionality: the playable game elements have been elided, leaving only a scrolling background of white cartoon clouds. The sense of rupture in comparing these two otherwise superficially similar glitches of technology lies with the distinction between a glitch that renders the work recognizably *non-functional* and a glitch that transforms the work into something recognizable but *afunctional*—without the capacity for the original function.

A critical role for glitch in creating a politically engaged media work requires *the glitch to make the political economy that produced the work that is failing to become apparent*. This meaning is not dependent on the use of the glitch *qua* glitch, but rather on the internal semiosis of the art object as understood by the audience. For the productive dimensions that create the work—its physicality, the material supports required for the production, the economic costs associated with that facture, distribution and presentation—to emerge *only* happens to the extent that those aspects of its production are the focus of the work itself: it is a question of content and context, not form. Only when glitched works are understood as displaying this alterity do they offer potentials for dissent—both aesthetic and political—a matter of how the audience interprets the human-readable work. The foregrounding of the technical failures in a recognizable fashion in *Untitled Game* assumes the readily recognized form of the non-functional. By enabling the potential interpretation of "broken," it enables the rejection of any critical meaning through the potential *recognition* that it is "broken."

Within a glitched work (glitch art) the *un*glitch has the same disruptive potential as a glitch in an otherwise normal work, as the conclusion of *Digital TV Dinner* shows. It is equally capable of bringing the critical dimensions of media practice to the attention of the audience, as a violation not only of established *a priori* expectations, but of the semiosis internal to the audience's engagement (not the digital facture). It is this ambivalence that offers the potential for these eruptions of criticality: the capacity of the glitch to become a redirection of meaning. However, these "openings" depend on an audience primed for such an encounter, and engaged with a work already placed within a context (such as that of art) where this critical meaning can develop. The functionality of a critical context does not necessarily result in a critical interpretation; not all interpretations developing from within such a space will necessarily be critical. The choice to produce an engaged, critical interpretation is made by the audience: there is always the potential for any work to be engaged as distraction (entertainment product), just as there is always the potential for a critical response to even the most banal narrative entertainment.

While the glitch can be an interruption of the perfect flow of media, these flows do not exist in actuality—in their place is the elision provided by the aura of the digital that creates this particular illusion. The conception of *any* glitch as inherently critical ignores the internalized procedures of elision (the aura of the digital) that accompany these illusions and are the defining features of both the glitch and the norm in digital media. A work organized *as critical* offers an expanded consideration for active spectators because of the ways it introduces the glitched elements, organizes them within the whole, and then enables a consideration of the relationship between the glitched and the norm. It is this tension between the expected form of the work (past experience) and the immanent example (encounter with a human-readable form) that identifies the critical mode and offers the *potential* for a critically oriented practice. Ambivalences are inherent to this type of interpretation: this critical mode suggests an excess apart from the observable content of the work, but dependent on what is observable in that work. The role of glitches within an engaged media practice is neither a purely formal experiment in technological failure, nor a stylistic decoration that enlivens otherwise banal work, but rather an interpretation where the disembodied technological instrumentalism of the digital that is otherwise being elided from conscious consideration through the linked illusions of perfection, transparency and immediacy becomes apparent.

What is most apparent about glitch is the enduring constraint posed by digital capitalism. A critical media praxis must therefore also contain a robust theoretical foundation that acknowledges and recognizes the traps posed by the digital: the interpreting audience will actively assimilate any technical failures into the normative form of the media being examined. This integration is what the aura of the digital describes. Critical meanings function only so long as the role of audience in encountering the work acknowledges the contingency of their interpretations: the critique of digital media employing glitch becomes tautologically entangled with the result. Digital technology as a whole represents the reification and disappearance of human interpretations from consideration. The inescapability of this loop is challenged only through the forced intrusion of those elements that are conceptually ignored: not in the material form of the work, but through its capacity for intellectualization. A shift in focus from the activities of the artist in making the work to the immanent ambiguities of interpretation may be the *only* means to constructing critical works. There is no easy or simple solution to this problem; simply employing *glitch* in media work does not automatically produce a critical meaning or render it critical.

Notes

1. Etcoff, Nancy. *Survival of the Prettiest: The Science of Beauty* (New York: Anchor Books, 1999) p. 217.
2. Larkin, Brian. "Degraded Images, Distorted Sounds: Nigerian Video and the Infrastructure of Piracy" in *Public Culture*, Vol. 16, No. 2 (2004) p. 291.
3. Kelly, Caleb. *Cracked Media: The Sound of Malfunction* (New Haven: MIT Press, 2009) pp. 59–60.
4. Larkin, Brian. "Degraded Images, Distorted Sounds: Nigerian Video and the Infrastructure of Piracy" in *Public Culture*, Vol. 16, No. 2 (2004) p. 292.
5. Menkman, Rosa. *Network Notebooks 4: The Glitch Moment(um)* (Amsterdam: Institute of Network Cultures, 2011) p. 35.
6. Gray, Cleve. "'The Great Spectator' interview" in *Art in America*, Vol. 57, No. 4 (July–August, 1969) p. 21.
7. Eco, Umberto. "Serial Form" in *The Limits of Interpretation* (Bloomington: University of Indiana Press, 1994) pp. 83–100.

Glossary

Artists producing visual glitches have engaged in a limited range of protocols for their creations and deployment in their work. This glossary provides a general framework for considering the types of manipulation and their relationship to the digital technology that produces the work. The production of glitches falls into five general categories that begin with the digital file itself and progress towards the physical presentation of the work, shifting from a manipulation of the virtual, digital instructions that are the file towards the literal presentation of that file for an audience.

(1) Data Manipulation

Data manipulation covers a range of approaches and protocols, all of which are focused on the transformation and alteration of the digital file itself: its dataset is changed to induce aberrant results when played normally on a computer. These varieties of glitching are the most immediately recognized as being *glitch,* and are readily apparent as specific, named protocols such as "datamoshing" in which a video file compressed using MPEG-1 has crucial image data removed (the I-frames), resulting in a cascading failure as the motion data is not refreshed with corresponding image data; Murata's *Monster Movie* employed this technique to produce its distinctive effects. Other variants of data manipulation, such as "data bending" involve the introduction of transient errors into the datastream that also produce cascading failures. The occasional "drop-outs" in digital video feeds (commonly seen during bad weather) are common examples of these transformations. Direct transformations of data to introduce errors and overflows when the file is rendered for a human audience overlap with transformations of the data using incorrect and inappropriate software, resulting in convergent results when encountered in human readable form.

(2) Misalignment

Misalignment between a digital file and the software that reads that file has two mirror-like variants: the first produces errors through the inappropriate application of decompression by decoding of a compressed file using an incorrect codec, resulting in a transformation of the encoded data, but without damaging the file itself; the second involves the induced opening/reading of a file using an incorrect software application. For example, opening a motion-encoded video file as audio, manipulating the audio-version of the dataset, then engaging the results either as audio, or returning it to be video again. Both these approaches involve mismatches between encoded data and its decoding, resulting in aberrant results when rendered for a human audience. Menkman's glitch-generating software *Monglot* creates its effects through the misalignment of encoded data with the codec for decoding it.

(3) Hardware Failure

Familiar from electronic music, the most famous type of hardware failure is "circuit bending," the creation of short circuits and physical "failures" in the hardware that renders electronic signals for a human audience. These physical failures in the technology itself (as distinct from software) produce glitches and aberrant results without necessarily altering the digital files being presented. The protocols used in the production of Fenton's *Digital TV Dinner* are examples of this physical engagement with technology that induces a glitch.

(4) Misregistration

The noise of historically analog recording technologies—the dirt, scratches, smudges and markings that can distort physical media also impact the playback of digital recordings on media such as CDs and DVDs where the data is accessed physically rather than electronically. The same physical interruptions that impact analog recordings can also distort and interrupt digital recordings that are physically stored. Most familiar from electronic music at the start of the twenty-first century, this approach to glitching engages the interface between the physical storage of the data and the data itself. The material markers of celluloid film that feature prominently in structural and materialist films of the 1960s-1970s involve the inclusion of this noise in the presentation itself.

(5) Distortion

Physical malfunctions of/in the presentation itself—problems with video screens, optical misalignments and electronic failures in video projectors for example are all physical failures that manifest as a distortion of the resulting presentation without altering or impacting the data itself. These mechanical faults and failings are the most common, and at the same time, the most transient. They reside in the particular device itself rather than being a feature of the data displayed. The earliest varieties of glitch belong to this category of failure: the RCA repair manuals published in the 1950s are concerned with the correction and identification of these physical failures in the display itself.

Glitch techniques align with particular sites of technological manipulation, yet all of them share an underlying engagement with the unexpected and aberrant behaviors of machinic systems proceeding autonomously. It is this particular engagement with the system as a such as it fails—no matter the particulars of that breakdown—that defines glitch techniques as an ongoing process of investigation, whatever the human readable form might be.

Index

abstraction: and capitalism 8, 11, 98; "The Idea of Abstraction" 54; parallels between painting and media 32, 62–3, 69–71; procedural 23, 36, 99; and realism (depiction) 54, 59, 75–6
Adorno, Theodor: "bourgeois functionalism" 128; inherent criticality 129
Ainsworth, Dick 23–6, 34
alienation 12, 100
American Federation of the Arts 52
Amerika, Mark 87–8
appropriation 7, 87, 90, 93
Archangel, Cory 21, 130
Arts and Crafts movement 8, 61
Atari 2600 Video Computer System 24
Attali, Jacques 6–7

Bally Astrocade 24–5, 28–9, 31–2, 34–5, 39–42, 44–6
Barker, Tim 15–16, 56
Barry, David 3
Bazin, André 52–6, 115
Bell Labs 28
Brakhage, Stan 35
Bridle, James 88, 94
broken 39, 45–6, 64, 102–4, 108, 130–1
Brown, Sheldon 29–30, 35
Burger, Peter 59
Burke, Edmond 116–18; *see also Decasia*

CableTV 27
capitalism 7–8, 13, 27; digital capitalism 8–17, 59–61, 89–91, 94–5, 123–7, 131; Marxist critique 8–12, 49, 57–9, 74–5; mystification 45–6, 64
Carroll, Noel 69–71
Carson, David 89
Casone, Kim: "The Aesthetics of Failure: 'Post-Digital' Tendencies in Contemporary Music" 3
Cavell, Stanley 52
Chicago 22–5
Clair, Patrick *see Halt and Catch Fire*
Cloninger, Curt 92–2
Constructivism 32–3
Contemporary art 14–15, 22, 76, 90–1
control revolution 10
Crow, Thomas 90
cybernetics *see* Taylor, Frederick W.

Decasia (2002) 113–22
DeFanti, Tom 23–5, 28, 30–1, 34
degrees of freedom 15–16, 31–2, 34–5, 37–8
Dieter, Michael 3
digital: "aura of information" 7–8, 80–1, 84–5, 92, 96, 126–7; "aura of the digital" 7–16, 45–6, 59–61, 64–5, 80, 86–7, 94–100, 102, 106–7, 112–13, 127, 131–2; as datastream 81, 85, 94–9, 133; fragmentation 3, 12–13, 32, 93, 100, 115, 125; ideal form 99; immaterialism 94–5; "on demand" generation 59–60, 80–1, 91–2, 96, 126–7; technical failure 3–5, 9, 21–3, 29–31, 46, 49–57,

60–61, 65–7, 72–6, 82, 86–92, 95–6, 99–100, 103, 108–12, 122, 125–31
Digital TV Dinner (1978/79) 22–46, 54, 63–7, 70, 83, 107, 125, 130, 134; *see also Bally Astrocade*
Donato, Nola 28
Duchamp, Marcel 21, 37–8, 44–5, 129; and *Erratum Musicale* 37–8, 44–5; and *Fountain* 129

Eisenstein, Sergei 74–5; *see also* montage
Electronic Visualization Event 3 (EVE3) 25, 29–30
Electronic Visualization Laboratory 23, 29
expanded cinema 1, 81–7

Fenton, Jay 22–5, 27–8, 29–32, 34, 38–40
film: found footage film 32–3, 40, 49, 113–14; structural film 51–3, 55, 65; *see also* materialist film
"film as film" 50–3, 71, 82, 103–4
Fischinger, Oskar 30
formalism 9–10, 52–3, 61, 63, 74, 95, 122, 128–9

Gidal, Peter 51, 53–4, 56–7, 60–1; *see also* materialist film
glitch: afunctionality 130; databending 96–8; datamoshing 36, 76, 99, 133; idealized 6, 8, 16, 95; as immanent encounter 7, 63–4, 99–100, 125; as material demonstration 7, 76, 126; music 1–2, 3–6, 9, 22–3; and performance 35, 37–8, 105; and video art 2, 9, 13–14, 22–4, 27, 29–30, 36, 50; and video games 130
glitch art: definition 22–3; "glitch-alike" 87
Grafix 28
Greenberg, Clement 11–13, 52–3, 61–2, 128
guerrilla television 27

Halley, Peter 105–6
Hallock-Greenewalt, Mary 21, 30
hallucination 66–70, 91
Halt and Catch Fire (2014) 103, 108–12, 113, 118
Hanhardt, John G. 52–3
Hatfield, Jackie 52
heuristics 1, 10–11, 50, 129
Höller, Christian 108
Hummel, Ernest 93

IDN magazine 2, 88
Ikeda, Ryoji 6–7
Image Union 23, 25–7, 28
invisibility 7
iterative completeness 34–6, 37–8

Jodi (the artist duo Joan Heemskerk and Dirk Paesmans) 21, 22–3; and *Untitled Game* 103–4, 130
Johnson, C.B. 14–15, 17, 51, 89–91

Kelly, Caleb 9, 125–6
Kolozova, Katerina 8–9, 10, 11
Kotik, Peter 38, 45

Larkin, Brian 123–4, 126
LeGrice, Malcolm 50, 53, 70–1
Levy, Malcom 3–4
Light Cone 108
Loos, Adolph 58–9, 128
Lukàcs, George 59
Lyotard, Francois 64–6

malfunction 2–3, 44–5, 56, 95, 97
Manon, Hugh S. 95–6, 99, 112
Marcuse, Herbert 59–60
Marks, Raul 109
materialist film 50–3, 65–9, 72, 75–6, 81–2, 103–5, 121–2, 128; characteristics 60
McEvilley, Thomas 61–3
McLaren, Norman 30, 34
Menkman, Rosa 50–1, 57, 87, 88–91, 99, 103–5, 127–8, 134
metaphysics 69, 71–2
*mis*function 17, 31, 44–5, 85–6
modernism: and anti-decoration 57–8; and the Contemporary 9–11, 14–17, 90–1; and film 69–70
montage 87, 90, 93, 107, 113, 115–19
Moradi, Iman 3, 32, 50, 57
Morris, Michael 81–6, 98–9
Morrison, Bill *see Decasia*
Murata, Takeshi 36, 76, 99–100, 133

new aesthetic 2, 76, 88, 94–5
noise 4–6, 15–16, 21, 23, 35, 39, 53, 60, 84–5, 87, 88, 102–3, 109–10, 127, 134; and nervous system 67, 69–71; in signal::noise 49
NTSC (video standard) 24

ontology 52–3, 55, 56–7, 100–1
optical sound 34, 82–3, 85–6
Oster, Gerald 67–9

Paik, Nam June 21, 30
paralogy: and critical media 64–5; definition 64; meaning::ambiguity 75, 106; and transgression 66–7, 68, 89
Paul, Christiane 3
phosphenes: definition 67; and flicker film 69–70; in meditation 70–1; and prisoner's cinema 69–72
Plato: allegory of the cave 66
Poggioli, Renato 12
postdigital aesthetics 3
Pure Data (Pd) 84–6

Ramey, Kathryn 35–6
Ray, Man 35
reappropriation *see* appropriation
recoding 123–5, 126, 128–9
reMI (Renate Oblak and Michael Pinter): and *zijkfijergijok* 107–8, 112, 125, 129
Russell, Catherine 86–7

Sacks, Oliver 66
Sandin, Dan 22–3, 28, 29–30, 34
Sandin Image Processor (IP) 22, 27, 29, 31, 35
Schein 59–60
Schwartz, Lillian 28, 34
scientific management 10–13
Scott, Ant 32
semiotic function 62, 75, 96; signifier of failure 112; signifier of rupture (criticality) 60–1, 113
Shamberg, Michael 27
Sharits, Paul 53, 82
Sitney, P. Adams 51–7
Solondz, Joshua Gen 65

Taylor, Frederick W. (Taylorism) 10–12, 57–8, 63
telediagraph 93
Temkin, Daniel 95–8, 99, 112

VanDerBeek, Stan 28
Vertov, Dziga 114
video processing 21–2, 30, 111
Virilio, Paul 112
visual music 21–3, 29–30, 31, 34, 38, 43–4, 63, 66, 81, 83, 118

Walley, Jonathan 82–3
Weinberg, Tom 27
white cube 59–60
Whitney, John 28
Wikipedia 23
Wilfred, Thomas 21, 30

YouTube 23–5

Zaritsky, Raul 23–4, 25, 27, 29

For Product Safety Concerns and Information please contact our EU representative GPSR@taylorandfrancis.com
Taylor & Francis Verlag GmbH, Kaufingerstraße 24, 80331 München, Germany

www.ingramcontent.com/pod-product-compliance
Lightning Source LLC
LaVergne TN
LVHW012333100826
845148LV00017B/2132

* 9 7 8 0 3 6 7 8 8 4 2 4 6 *